Praise for *First, Fast, Fearless* by Ed Hiner

"I challenge you to read and absorb every word of this book. It's a revolution. It's an inspiration. And it will be your ally when you inevitably march into the battles of business and life."

> —from the Foreword by Ken Blanchard, coauthor
> of *The New One Minute Manager* and *Leading at a Higher Level*

"Selfless leadership is the explosive power that drives the world's most elite teams. In *First, Fast, Fearless*, Ed Hiner shows us how to tap into that power by revealing the hidden forces elite leaders harness to drive mission success. Indispensable!"

> —Tony Robbins, #1 *New York Times* bestselling author

"If you want a tough, wise, and battle-tested coach who can help you to become a better leader, then dive into *First, Fast, Fearless*. In it, Iron Ed uses real-life experiences to teach us about the art of leadership. Read this book, and you'll have an impact on the teams that you lead."

> —Eric Greitens, Navy SEAL Lieutenant Commander
> and *New York Times* bestselling author of *The Heart and the Fist* and *Resilience*

"Ed Hiner has accomplished the difficult task of writing a book that both instructs and entertains. His career as a U.S. Navy SEAL serves as a rich resource for proven leadership techniques equally applicable to civilian world scenarios. Vignettes from the author's operational experiences liven up the solid leadership lessons. *First, Fast, Fearless: How to Lead Like a Navy SEAL* will significantly improve your leadership capabilities and enhance the productivity of your team."

> —Rear Admiral John F. Calhoun (ret.), former commander of the USS *Constellation*

"Focus in the ever-changing environment of business is essential. In *First, Fast, Fearless*, Ed Hiner distills powerful leadership lessons forged in the crucible of combat that will help any leader develop the frontline focus and first strike mindset required for business success."

> —Garry Ridge, president and CEO of WD-40 Company

"Ed Hiner redefines what successful leadership means in the twenty-first century. His inspirational stories of struggle, triumph, and brotherhood as a Lt. Commander in the U.S. Navy SEALs define what it takes for people to successfully lead high-performance teams during good and bad times. With the right mindset, discipline, and compassion, Ed reminds us that anyone can become a fearless leader. His candor, compassion, and insights into what it takes to be a transformational leader are a must-read for anyone aspiring to lead high-performance teams."

—Claudia San Pedro, CFO of SONIC, America's Drive-In

"In his years as an elite special forces leader, Ed Hiner lived and breathed the principles of authentic leadership and followership, which he distills in these pages. Riveting and inspiring, *First, Fast, Fearless* is essential reading for business leaders who want to up their game and play at the elite level."

— David Swanson, EVP of HR at SAP/SuccessFactors

"Ed Hiner's leadership is so outstanding, I wrote about him in *The Sheriff of Ramadi*. Ed is the real deal, and he's brought his combat leadership and warrior ethos experience together in this terrific book. Recommended reading for anyone who wishes to excel, *First, Fast, Fearless* is inspirational and speaks to the warrior in all of us."

—Dick Couch, Navy SEAL (ret.) and bestselling author
of *The Warrior Elite* and *Chosen Soldier*

"Iron Ed Hiner is a leadership guru. In *First, Fast, Fearless*, he weaves fascinating stories from his 20-year career as a Navy SEAL into powerful leadership maxims for us all. A must-read for any business leader—and those who aspire to leadership."

—John R. Driscoll, SVP of finance at General Atomics

"Ed Hiner's leadership and wisdom brought many SEALs through the fire and back home; I was one of them. This book will be a great guide to military and civilian leaders alike. With these powerful words, Ed continues to bring us home to this day."

—Kristin Beck, Navy SEAL Senior Chief (ret.) and subject of *Lady Valor*

"As a college baseball player, I once had a friend, classmate, and teammate by the name of Ed Hiner. Many years later, it's easy to recall his best traits: energy, work ethic, positivity, and toughness . . . along with a touch of power from the left side of the plate! Most of all, Ed was the embodiment of a great teammate, which is clearly a trait he has maintained throughout his life. Like me, I believe you will find this book to be an inspirational read that exemplifies the passion, courage, and all-around leadership required of the First, Fast, and Fearless."

—Jerry Dipoto, GM of the Los Angeles Angels

"Ed Hiner tells it like it is. A great read for leaders who want to be among the elite."

—Representative Ryan Zinke (R-Montana), Navy SEAL Commander (ret.) and former Deputy and acting Commander of Combined Joint Special Operations Task Force–Arabian Peninsula

"Ed artfully connects the dots and shows how to take the essential principles forged by the greatest leadership laboratory on earth, the Navy SEALs, and make them a way of life. A must-read for emerging leaders."

—Doyle N. Beneby, CEO of CPS Energy

"The lessons that lead to consistently excellent results for our heroes are equally valuable in the business world. *First, Fast, Fearless* provides the inspiration and practical framework to build a leadership style that works. This will transform your life and the way you lead."

—Robert Goodman, president of FortéONE

"Lt. Commander Hiner does a brilliant job of taking the SEAL Ethos and weaving it into a superb blueprint on leadership as applicable in the boardroom and in our personal lives as on the battlefield. Everything is anchored to the ethos as Ed discusses building trust, problem solving, teamwork and how these apply across all spectrums of our lives. His commentary on humility as a key trait in great leaders is particularly inspiring and the profound impact leaders have on the stress level of their troops or employees is a real eye-opener. You cannot compare what we do as business leaders to the responsibilities of our heroes in the military, but the parallels Ed draws in terms of the practical and tactical aspects of leadership are uncanny and serve as a valuable path to success."

—Robert A. Sullivan, president of Fifth Third Bank, Chicago

"Ed Hiner shows us how authentic leadership goes far beyond 'winning.' It can actually be the solution to dilemmas faced by the top echelon of the corporate world. His words have a fierce intensity that resonate with those who are responsible for the lives of others—on the battlefield, in business, or elsewhere. Developed from a deep understanding of how good leaders impact the outcome of life and death decisions, Hiner guides us through the building blocks of a steadfast determination to get the job done, powered by honor, discipline, and adherence to only the highest principles."

—Christina de Vaca, director of the Master of Science in Executive Leadership program at the University of San Diego

"Most of us are fascinated by (and grateful to) the Navy SEALs. "Iron Ed" Hiner's book offers not only a behind the scenes look at these warriors but, more important, a nuanced picture of what they are really like. Most important, he offers powerful leadership lessons that anyone charged with achieving goals through others can adopt and emulate. A bonus: the book is a quick and interesting read!"

—B. Joseph White, James F. Towey Professor of Business and Leadership and president emeritus of the University of Illinois and author of *The Nature of Leadership*

"I sat on the bench for nearly two decades, and I believe that First, Fast, Fearless leadership has the potential to change our world for the better. It is the best leadership book I have ever read."

—Anthony J. Heckemeyer, Senior Circuit Judge, Missouri

"How refreshing to read a leadership book that reflects on the rigors of business, with all of its stresses, using military leadership techniques. Those of us raised in military families can completely relate to the bar this leadership way of life sets. The bar is high, and what it can create in building a team in the workplace is completely worth taking the time to implement. I will be using the tools provided here personally and within my business."

—Christy Cardillo, CPA, partner at Shinn and Company, LLC

"Ed Hiner has nailed what it takes to lead in VUCA situations, which is today's environment. If you want to lead an organization that has a strong sense of mission and esprit de corps, read this book. Your employees may never be cold, wet, and uncomfortable in the work setting, but this book will help you develop the first strike capability to create enduring success. It should be on the reading list of every business leader, MBA program, and military organization."

—Colonel Ray Bender (ret.), PhD, coauthor of *Culture.com* and *I Should Be Burnt Out by Now . . . So How Come I'm Not?*

First, Fast, Fearless

HOW TO LEAD LIKE A
NAVY SEAL

BRIAN "IRON ED" HINER
NAVY SEAL LIEUTENANT COMMANDER (RET.)

Mc
Graw
Hill
Education

NEW YORK   CHICAGO   SAN FRANCISCO   ATHENS
LONDON   MADRID   MEXICO CITY   MILAN
NEW DELHI   SINGAPORE   SYDNEY   TORONTO

1 2 3 4 5 6 7 8 9 0   QFR/QFR   1 2 1 0 9 8 7 6 5

ISBN 978-0-07-184488-8
MHID   0-07-184488-0

e-ISBN 978-0-07-184481-9
e-MHID   0-07-184481-3

Design by Mauna Eichner and Lee Fukui

McGraw-Hill Education books are available at special quantity discounts to use as premiums and sales promotions or for use in corporate training programs. To contact a representative, please visit the Contact Us pages at www.mhprofessional.com.

To my son, Jake, and wife, Wendy,
the treasure of my life

Contents

CONTENTS

PART II
RUNNING TO THE SOUND OF GUNFIRE
The Essence of Brotherhood

PART III

BATTLE RHYTHM
Turning Brand and Brotherhood into Music

Foreword

When I was a young boy, I read comic books. Lots of them. One of my heroes was Superman. I'm sure you've heard of him—he's still around today. For a brief time in my early years, I believed that he was real. An actual living superhero. Eventually, I realized that the Man of Steel and his alter-ego, mild-mannered reporter Clark Kent, were nothing more than the invention of Jerry Siegel's and Joe Shuster's creative minds. Since that time—all through junior high, high school, and college—my only real superheroes were my mother, Dorothy Blanchard, and my father, Ted Blanchard. My dad was an Admiral in the U.S. Navy, and he, along with my mom, taught me values that I have never forgotten nor neglected. Things such as love of God and country, integrity, respect for others, generosity, and the sheer joy of learning.

Then without warning, along came another kind of superhero. Another man who loved God and country, who had integrity, who respected others, who gave of himself, and who loved everything about learning. This man was a student of mine at the University of San Diego (USD). He was in my classes. He was pursuing his master's degree in executive leadership, part of a program that we had developed with the USD faculty for their School of Business. He seemed like an ordinary guy, interested in learning and leading. Little did I know that he was already a significant, established leader.

This student was training elite teams and then leading them into battle—where they could easily lose their lives.

Now, I don't know about you, but in all my years of leading—and teaching leadership skills to others through books and classes and lectures—I have never told anyone, "Follow me, and, by the way, you could die." What teacher, what trainer, what corporate executive or nonprofit CEO asks that of the people he or she leads?

Well, Ed Hiner did exactly that. He lived by a code that few of us can comprehend. Ed, now retired, was a U.S. Navy SEAL for 20 years. He led brave people into battle—in Iraq, in Afghanistan, and in many other hostile places around the world—fighting odds that we can't possibly imagine. And he won.

I believe that the reason he won is that he knew some secrets that few others have discovered. One of those secrets? He knew that stress is a killer. It doesn't just lead to heart attacks or PTSD. It leads to underperformance, indecision, and on-the-job misery. He also knew that, among the many external and internal factors that lead to stress, poor leaders do the most damage. He knew that while some stress is good—it helps keep us sharp and focused—too much of the wrong kind of stress can actually destroy high-performing organizations, whether they be military units, corporations, educational institutions, nonprofits—even families. These are the things that "Iron Ed" can teach you.

I challenge you to read and absorb every word of this book. It's a revolution. It's an inspiration. And it will be your ally when you inevitably march into the battles of business and life.

In some ways, I was Ed Hiner's teacher. And I'm proud that I can say that. But in many more ways, "Iron Ed" was my teacher. I'm pleased that I can say that!

—KEN BLANCHARD

Acknowledgments

I cannot take all the credit for the content in this book. Leadership is learned. Without all the great leaders and teammates whom I was fortunate enough to learn from, I would have had very little to write, so thank you to every one of my teammates. I would like to thank each of you by name, but many of you are still out there doing the job as we sleep safe in our beds at night.

Putting the words "Navy SEAL" on the cover of this leadership book came with a profound responsibility because of the respect and love that I have for my brothers in the SEAL Teams. My intent was to make you proud and to honor a great group of warriors and human beings for all that you have done and continue to do. I hope I have succeeded.

Navy SEALs do not have a patent on leadership, courage, or any other virtue, for that matter. I would like to thank all of the men and women of the U.S. Armed Forces who have served and continue to serve a cause greater than themselves. I've seen great acts of courage and compassion in some of the most dangerous places in the world by warriors from all branches of service. No one will ever know how much you have done. Thank you to all my brothers and sisters in uniform, past, present, and future.

I would like to thank my wife and swim buddy, Wendy, and my son, Jake, for believing and trusting in me as I transitioned out of the SEAL Teams. I also want to thank you for patiently listening to the same ideas over and over again until I got them right.

Military service, especially during times of war, puts a heavy strain on the families of those who serve, so I would like to thank my extended family: the Driscolls, Hiners, Borkums, Greenwalds, and all the military families of service members. I would like to thank my "outlaws," John and MaryAnn Driscoll, for their support and the comfort it gave me, knowing they would be there to take care of my wife and son if I didn't come home.

Mom, Pops, and Peg, thanks for believing in an "ole country boy" from the Blue Ridge Mountains of Virginia. Pops, I'm sorry you are not around to see the book on the shelf, but I know you had confidence in me and would be very proud.

I would like to acknowledge the families of all the men and women who gave the ultimate sacrifice and did not come home. They are a significant part of the newest and greatest generation.

In the book, I have a few stories that involve Matt Hecke-meyer, who became my best friend the day we met. Thank you, Matt, for being there, for being my best friend, and for never telling me "I told you so" about the book.

My friends and mentors, Gail Brooks and Ken Jackson, thank you for being in my corner for over 20 years and constantly encouraging me in everything I've done.

As a new officer, it is important to have a good first example to follow. I was very fortunate to have a great first example of leadership and friendship, so thank you, Rhett Fisher.

Admiral Jack Calhoun, thank you for believing in me and helping me get the opportunity to become an officer in the SEAL Teams.

I am very fortunate to have the best publisher in the business, so thank you to my editor, Casey Ebro, at McGraw-Hill and to the whole McGraw-Hill staff, for believing in me and being patient with me through the process.

To my colleague Peter Sander: thank you for helping bring this project to life by being the professional that you are.

To my agent, Frank Weimann: thank you for being a straight shooter and for helping to put this project together.

To Ken and Margie Blanchard and the Ken Blanchard Companies: thank you for everything you have done to help others and to help me see the possibilities of true leadership.

Lastly, I would like to thank all the readers and leaders who are willing to pick up this book and read a different perspective on leadership with the openness of learning something new and becoming a better leader and, hopefully, a better person.

Becoming a Leader of Leaders

L ate one evening in early May 2011, the President of the United States held a televised news conference to announce the killing of the world's number one terrorist: Osama bin Laden. As we all know now, U.S. Navy SEALs were the tip of the spear of that operation.

Since early on in America's war on terrorism, we've heard stories of great heroism by American forces, and Navy SEALs in particular. Navy SEALs have a reputation for getting the most difficult missions done. But they're also known for their extreme standards of physical and mental toughness, strength, endurance, and agility. Some SEALs have risen into the national consciousness through books and movies, including *Lone Survivor*, *No Easy Day*, and *American Sniper*. All give great accounts of heroic Americans in action.

But they don't tell the whole story.

That's where *First, Fast, Fearless* comes in. I am a Navy SEAL Officer, retired from 20 years of active duty in both leader and follower roles. I have risen from being the lowest-ranking member of a platoon to being the Commanding Officer of an entire Task Unit at war. I've seen it all, and I want to tell the whole story. I want to tell the story of leadership in the extremes and how that leadership paradigm can work for you in civilian life.

Beyond extreme physical and combat achievements, we SEALs are also known for mental toughness, bias for action, decisiveness, creative thinking, adaptability, and perseverance—all under extreme stress. Yet apart from the image of the "steely-eyed killer"—thanks in part to those books and movies, among others, mentioned above—SEALs also have a deeply human, values-driven, and virtuous side. We get things done through, by, and with others, and we rely on a strong foundation of honesty and trust. These qualities—all found in the world's most effective leaders—afford a unique and effective way of doing what others cannot.

Leading units into battle requires more than just elite warriors. It requires elite *leaders* to build elite organizations beforehand. Behind the tip of the spear, there are hundreds performing different jobs and dedicated to the mission. The challenge is clear: How do we take on complex, ambiguous, volatile, and dangerous operations that bring so many together from all parts of the military? How do we approach such extreme missions and dangers while keeping everyone—and everything—flying in formation? The answers lie herein.

Great leadership matters. And every leader can benefit from the First, Fast, Fearless leadership that we hone in the SEAL Teams.

First, Fast, Fearless Leadership Makes It Happen

The 9/11 terrorist attacks brought about a period of great stress for U.S. Navy SEALs, with continuous combat deployments around the globe. No other time in American history has involved Special Operations warriors in sustained combat for so long. Yet, in the face of such adversity, SEALs have enjoyed the highest retention rate anywhere in the military. We continue to be resilient and flourish in environments most people cannot imagine.

But *First, Fast, Fearless* isn't a book about war. It doesn't glamorize war, bravery, or any actions of my own. I've had my fair share of war, felt my fair share of hurt, experienced my fair share of stress, and seen my fair share of failures and setbacks.

The intent of *First, Fast, Fearless* is to capture the essence of true leadership, a leadership style and brand carefully honed and forged from years of SEAL experience and determination under stress. It's a system that works, and I believe it works equally well on the battlefield or in the boardroom—or anywhere in between.

Stress Got You Down? Try Good Leadership.

Six years after 9/11, I became the Training and Readiness Officer for all SEAL Teams on the West Coast. It was my job to ensure that people were trained and ready to deploy in all physical and psychological aspects. I helped build a resilience program to better understand and resolve pressures confronting the force.

For this program, we held a week-long off-site conference. The working group included about 70 SEALs of different ranks across the community. The goal was to identify the stresses we face and how to reduce them. One big takeaway was the importance of taking an offensive mindset—a central theme of First, Fast, Fearless leadership.

The off-site group also recognized the effects of leadership on resilience, retention, productivity, and overall morale. Leadership emerged as the main topic of discussion for the entire week. Leadership, initially regarded as a "stressor," came to be regarded as the "answer."

By the end of the week, it was unanimous: leadership was the thread that tied everything together across the force. We could identify where bad leadership had devastated SEAL Teams. We charted deployments, considering for each one the person in charge, how that team did overseas, the retention rate, and how team members bounced back upon return. We didn't need PhDs to figure out the pattern: great leadership is critical in times of stress and fear. It stared us right in the face.

I began to research more deeply operational stressors and stress relief, and my research included work sessions with the

Walter Reed National Military Medical Center and a summit with the Naval Center for Combat and Operational Stress Control (COSC). A study by the Army's Mental Health Advisory Team (MHAT) IV on troops who had served in Iraq during Operation Iraqi Freedom from 2005 to 2007 leaped out at me.

Every soldier returning home completed an anonymous survey to identify possible stress-related disorders. The study showed that soldiers with high combat experience screened positive for post-traumatic stress disorder (PTSD) symptoms 20 percent of the time when they viewed their leaders favorably. When soldiers viewed their leaders unfavorably, the PTSD-positive rate jumped to 40 percent. A group of Marines tested PTSD positive 44 percent of the time under unfavorable leaders versus 19 percent of the time under favorable ones.

The takeaway: stress symptoms roughly double when the troops don't view their leadership favorably. Good leadership provides a protective influence to maintain mental health and well-being, even in the face of extreme combat.

Steely-Eyed Killers in Your Workplace

Though not a doctor, I have become something of an expert on PTSD through my SEAL experience. As I studied the effects of leadership on stress and PTSD, I came across a Washington, D.C., psychiatrist and specialist on the topic. She pointed out that most of her clients were businesspeople exhibiting many of the same stress symptoms as combat veterans. A bad boss, a toxic environment, fear of losing their job, marketplace uncertainty, and many other typical stressors of modern corporate life collectively produced enough stress to fill her office on a daily basis.

As you can imagine, being a SEAL subjects you to great amounts of stress and fear. Studies have shown that fear shuts down the executive part of your brain, the part responsible for imagination and problem solving. The brain doesn't know the difference between fear associated with a toxic leader and fear that a lion on the savannah may be stalking you. *First, Fast, Fearless* is meant to capture the leadership traits that most effectively deal with the fear and stress the environment puts on the team. *First, Fast, Fearless* is not, however, a quick-fix tool; rather, it portrays a leadership system, one that becomes a way of life.

Throughout my career, I've had the opportunity to work with great people and great leaders. SEALs and other Special Operations Forces have developed their leadership styles more deeply since 9/11 than in their prior history. Most were forged in the heat of battle where the stakes are highest. But I believe they carry over with great effect to the "business battlefield" as well. Many of the same issues and challenges are there, just without the bullets, bombs, and life-and-death choices evident in the military edition.

Leadership must be a way of life and must be driven by a strong ethos. The difference between authentic leadership and "demonstration leadership," usually an assertion of ego and power, is readily apparent to everyone on a team, especially in the heat of battle.

As you read, you'll come to see that military and nonmilitary situations are more similar than not when it comes to stress and leadership. The First, Fast, Fearless leadership style is effective in both contexts. With respect to leadership, our "steely-eyed killers" are really no different from you.

One final note: a lot of what happens in the life of a SEAL happens very fast and may occasionally be obscured by the fog of war. As such, what you read here is what I lived and learned to the best of my memory.

The First, Fast, Fearless Tour of Duty

It's time for a "direct action" assault into the world of First, Fast, Fearless leadership.

First, Fast, Fearless leadership, as we practice it on the SEAL Teams, is made up of three key elements: Brand, Brotherhood, and Battle Rhythm. Whether or not SEALs have direct reports, we are all leaders, and as such, we all develop these three attributes from day one.

Brand refers to your own personal leadership style. After committing to become a leader—or a leader of leaders—as a member of the SEAL Teams, you develop a style and Brand over time. The First, Fast, Fearless Brand includes a first strike mindset, an all-in commitment to ethos, a strong sense of humility and humanity, and an always-on nature, among other traits.

Part I, "Do Your Part First: The Brand of a True Leader," examines the essence of a strong First, Fast, Fearless leadership Brand—what it is, what it isn't, and how you get there.

Once Brand is established, the next critical element is *Brotherhood*. Among SEALs, little else comes through more clearly than the sense of sacrifice, teamwork, and mutual commitment we have to each other. Brotherhood is more than teamwork. It is always on, and it is directed by deep inner values far beyond simply collaborating and leveraging each other's capabilities.

Part II, "Running to the Sound of Gunfire: The Essence of Brotherhood," describes the true nature of First, Fast, Fearless–style Brotherhood—what makes it happen, what makes it tick, and how it's different from what you've probably experienced as a civilian.

Finally, while Brand and Brotherhood are critically important, they aren't sufficient to accomplish an important mission or goal. A musician can play music individually, but the impact of the music greatly expands when musicians play together in rhythm. A conductor sets an orchestra's rhythm. What we do in the SEAL Teams is more like jazz: we all have the rhythm in our heads to move forward as a team without the presence of a central commanding leader. I find such rhythm to be the highest essence of how the SEAL Teams work. To the extent that you can "play jazz" in the workplace, you'll get much further much faster, all with less fear and stress.

Part III, "Battle Rhythm: Turning Brand and Brotherhood into Music," explains how Battle Rhythm can become a regular part of your organizational life.

Before getting into the three parts, in Chapter 1 I take you through a short pretour basic training to describe what SEALs are and how people become SEALs, both of which set the stage for what follows.

HOOYAH!

A Special Kind of Warrior

The SEAL Ethos

In times of war or uncertainty there is a special breed of warrior ready to answer our Nation's call. A common man with uncommon desire to succeed. Forged by adversity, he stands alongside America's finest special operations forces to serve his country, the American people, and protect their way of life. I am that man.

My Trident is a symbol of honor and heritage. Bestowed upon me by the heroes that have gone before, it embodies the trust of those I have sworn to protect. By wearing the Trident I accept the responsibility of my chosen profession and way of life. It is a privilege that I must earn every day. My loyalty to Country and Team is beyond reproach. I humbly serve as a guardian to my fellow Americans always ready to defend those who are unable to defend themselves. I do not advertise the nature of my work, nor seek recognition for my actions. I voluntarily accept the inherent hazards of my profession, placing the welfare and security of others before my own. I serve with honor on and off the battlefield. The ability to control my emotions and my actions, regardless of circumstance, sets me apart from other men.

Uncompromising integrity is my standard. My character and honor are steadfast. My word is my bond.

We expect to lead and be led. In the absence of orders I will take charge, lead my teammates, and accomplish the mission. I lead by example in all situations. I will never quit. I persevere and thrive on adversity. My Nation expects me to be physically harder and mentally stronger than my enemies. If knocked down, I will get back up, every time. I will draw on every remaining ounce of strength to protect my teammates and to accomplish our mission. I am never out of the fight.

We demand discipline. We expect innovation. The lives of my teammates and the success of our mission depend on me—my technical skill, tactical proficiency, and attention to detail. My training is never complete. We train for war and fight to win. I stand ready to bring the full spectrum of combat power to bear in order to achieve my mission and the goals established by my country. The execution of my duties will be swift and violent when required yet guided by the very principles that I serve to defend. Brave men have fought and died building the proud tradition and feared reputation that I am bound to uphold. In the worst of conditions, the legacy of my teammates steadies my resolve and silently guides my every deed. I will not fail.

At the Underwater Demolition Team (UDT)/SEAL museum in Fort Pierce, Florida, stands the statue of a lone fighter, clad only in swim trunks, with no equipment other than his fins and dive mask. At his feet, he has a sack of explosives. When this lone man enters the water in the dark, he has nothing but the skills and values he has developed through his training. With the simplest equipment, he is deadly. These warriors swam onto the beaches of all the major landings in World War II. About 75 percent of them were either killed or wounded, and most people don't know they ever existed. Sailors on the ships thought the warriors were crazy and referred to them as "naked warriors." These were the archetypal frogmen, the predecessor to the Navy SEALs. Even today, we still call ourselves "frogmen" and "naked warriors."

SEAL stands for **Se**a, **A**ir, and **L**and. As the U.S. Navy's principal Special Operations Force, SEALs have evolved into one of the leading Special Operations Forces in the world. There are about 2,700 SEALs on active duty, around 1,200 of whom are engaged in frontline duty.

Navy SEALs are trained to operate in all environments—the sea, air, and land, for which we are named. We are trained to operate in climate extremes, including Arctic cold, scorching desert, and jungle environments. Our tasks include direct action, special reconnaissance, counterterrorist operations, foreign internal defense, and unconventional warfare. We also engage in counter-illegal-drug-trafficking operations and hostage and personnel recovery. Historically, we have had "one foot in the water," but more recently, many of our operations have occurred in the mountains and deserts of Iraq and Afghanistan.

Today, our business is wherever our country's need takes us.

What *Is* a Warrior Anyway?

You'd probably define a warrior as someone who fights in a war. However, the truer definition separates the warrior from the common soldier. A warrior is a specialist within the context of a tribal or clan-based society that recognizes a separate warrior class.

A warrior gets the job done, whether through direct combat or other means; the warrior sees the big picture and the greater good of his actions; the warrior seeks to win and to defeat, not necessarily to destroy. SEALs are an elite team of warriors who become part of the brotherhood because we want to belong and we want to succeed.

A warrior, in short, is a *leader.*

> **A mercenary does a job because he's paid to.**
> **A soldier does his because he's ordered to.**
> **A warrior does it because he *wants* to.**

The Core Ideas: Physical and Moral Courage, Teamability, and Problem Solving

It's not easy for us SEALs to describe ourselves. Unfortunately, the movie industry doesn't help much, for we are often portrayed as highly skilled killers capable of taking out our targets under extreme conditions. That's true. We can kill. Sometimes we have to, and we do it under adversity. But we're a whole lot more than that. We are leaders possessing traits of physical and moral courage, teamability, and problem solving, traits that we recruit for, select, and train into every SEAL. The SEAL Ethos encapsulates it far better than the movies do.

What are these special traits? In our context, the physical courage to be a warrior is obvious. Behind that, however, lies a deep well of moral courage—the honesty, humility, dependability, and emotional fortitude—that lead to trust and consistency of action. Moral courage and fortitude are as important as physical courage. If a person is untrustworthy under fire, he (see "What About Women?" later in the chapter) cannot be a SEAL.

You won't find the word *teamability* in the dictionary. It's the term we use to describe the ability to accept your role on the team and to place the team before yourself. We use the term and deploy the concept all the time. We reinforce teamwork and hold each SEAL and SEAL trainee accountable by assigning what we call a "swim buddy." A team player must be able to lead and to follow interchangeably.

SEALs also must have a natural ability to solve complex problems. We don't—and can't—train problem-solving ability into SEAL recruits. But we do test for the ability, and we build teams that foster individual ability to solve problems, which is what every leader should do.

A group of *physically* and *morally courageous* warriors acting together as a *team* to *problem solve* toward a stated mission or goal—that's who we SEALs really are. Whether in direct combat or helping others solve problems, we are all leaders—trained as leaders and engaged as leaders.

Let's Put a Man on the Moon. We Need SEALs Too.

How did we get from the naked warrior frogman to today's modern SEAL warrior?

I won't cover every step in the history of the SEAL Teams— our victories and conquests, changes in structure and leadership, and so forth. That can all be found easily on the Internet (the official Naval Special Warfare website at www.sealswcc.com is an excellent source). Our story is one of evolution to meet the rapidly changing circumstances and context of modern warfare.

In the 1961 speech in which he announced his plan to put a man on the moon, President John F. Kennedy, against the backdrop of guerilla warfare in Vietnam, also announced his intention to strengthen U.S. Special Forces and unconventional warfare capabilities. He created the first two SEAL Teams, which formally came to be in January 1962.

While this action launched the SEAL Teams, the idea of special operations was hardly new. Today's Navy SEALs can trace our roots to World War II, where at least four different groups of Special Forces played important roles in both the European and Pacific theaters, from reconnaissance to direct assistance with the beach landings on D-Day and on numerous Pacific islands, and other amphibious operations. These "ancestor" teams included the Special Service Units of the Scouts and Raiders beach reconnaissance teams, the Naval Combat Demolition Units who bravely demolished waterborne barriers in North Africa and Normandy, the Operational Swimmers of the Office of Strategic Services who pioneered much of today's underwater diving equipment, and the Navy Underwater Demolition Teams who saw World War II action primarily in the Pacific.

Kennedy's announcement formalized and gave visibility to something that had existed for 20 years, a Special Force for the future. Instead of several smaller forces within our major military branches, the SEALs would become the lead force to conduct highly skilled, low visibility operations with high strategic impact.

Today's SEALs operate within the U.S. Navy as part of the Naval Special Warfare Command and U.S. Special Operations Command, but occasionally they serve under or in cooperation with other operations such as the CIA's Special Operations Group. SEALs also team up with Special Forces from other countries, such as the British Special Forces.

Today there are eight "conventional" SEAL Teams based on two SEAL bases, one in Coronado, California, and the other in Little Creek (outside of Virginia Beach), Virginia. A more specialized team known as the Naval Warfare Special Development Group is now deployed for especially important and classified counterterrorist operations, such as the 2011 dispatch of Osama bin Laden. SEAL Special Vehicle Delivery Team 1 is another more specialized SEAL group.

Up until recently, most SEAL operations were just as one might expect—clandestine, low visibility, high impact, low publicity operations, such as clearing a beach of concrete barriers and mines for an amphibious landing. But as SEALs have been pulled into the highly charged nonconventional warfare theaters of Iraq and Afghanistan, we have gained a higher profile—not necessarily a good thing or desirable in special operations. SEALs were not only involved in the bin Laden takedown, the details of which have recently come to light, but were also involved in rescuing Captain Richard Phillips from Somalian pirates in the 2009 hijacking of the *Maersk Alabama* and the 2014 recapture of the tanker *My Morning Glory* in the Mediterranean.

Unlike businesses, we don't always thrive on publicity. We act as a team, not as a group of individuals, and we thrive on results, gained in a manner consistent with our ethos, not by making a public spectacle of our actions. As true leaders, we remain focused on the task, not on ourselves and our résumés. What it means to be a SEAL hasn't changed for us, despite greater world attention.

You're Tough, Brave, and Strong. What More Does It Take?

So you think *you* have trouble recruiting people with the "right stuff" for your organization? Try finding those special physically, mentally, and emotionally well-rounded individuals who are high-performing leaders but can also function within a team under extreme stress. Who are these people? Where do you find them? How do you develop them into fully successful warriors who can lead and be led with a "five-nines" level of trust into some of the world's most hostile places?

The process to become a SEAL is long and difficult. From the Basic Underwater Demolitions/SEAL (BUD/S) training until the first deployment takes 2½ years. Since the terrorist attacks on September 11, 2001, the highest-ranking officer in the Navy, the Chief of Naval Operations, has made recruiting SEALs his number one recruiting priority. This is significant, considering that the SEAL Teams compose only a small fraction of 1 percent of the Navy.

Selecting and Recruiting a SEAL

We knew that the war on terrorism would require many special operations, but we weren't a very big organization. We all know how important it is to get the right people first, so we had a team of analysts create a profile of the ideal SEAL candidate. We analyzed all the traits and characteristics of successful candidates and successful SEALs. Some of the results are obvious, like physicality, resilience, patriotism, and toughness. But some of the "signal" traits and characteristics we found were a bit surprising.

Yankees and Surfers

We found that candidates from New England had a higher success rate than those from any other portion of the country. The next successful group of candidates came from the north central and Great Plains portions of the western United States, states like North and South Dakota, Nebraska, Kansas, Minnesota, Iowa, and Missouri. Finally, the third most successful group originated from the north Pacific Coast: Washington, Oregon, and California.

It's not known exactly why those from these regions excel, but in my opinion, it has to do with the cold climate and the ability to endure physical and climate-affected hardship. While the West Coast is not considered cold, the *water* is—and many from the West Coast are cold-water surfers. Getting into 50-degree water at five in the morning builds physical and mental toughness. SEAL training has everything to do with being wet, cold, and uncomfortable.

And Wrestlers

Some of the traits that you might expect candidates to possess are a mission-driven, adaptive, and innovative mindset, superb fitness, a high level of intelligence, a team orientation, and a keen motivation to avoid "dull normalcy." Our candidates tend to play team sports, but interestingly, we found that many of our successful candidates were wrestlers.

If you have ever wrestled, you know that the training is very hard, strenuous, and painful. It takes a great deal of discipline to endure the physical training for wrestling and the limited calorie intake to maintain a lighter physique in order to wrestle the small-est person possible.

Chess Players Too!

Whenever we had visiting dignitaries, as the Training Officer in charge, I would brief them on the SEAL training program. With-out fail, each time, I surprised them with a fact they didn't expect: chess players were almost *four times* more likely to make it through training than non-chess players!

It should come as no surprise, really. SEALs need to be problem solvers who think strategically and often outside the box, to confront new problems in real time and think a few moves ahead through the solutions. SEALs are not the knuckle-dragging thugs some people believe us to be! We are thinkers and doers; as President Kennedy mandated, a force to go anywhere, anytime, and do anything.

This requires people able and willing to bend the rules and norms to get to someone else's king (or queen or even a pawn, as the strategic objective called for). "Rule bender" was another trait that we found highest among successful SEALs. Give me a mix of a problem solver and a rule bender, and you have an innovator. An innovator, in this arena? You bet. It's very important in our space, and it's part of our ethos, as you may have noticed at the beginning of the chapter.

How to Become a SEAL

It takes a year to be qualified as a SEAL, and 2½ years to be fully trained and ready for the first deployment. SEAL training is extremely rigorous, among the toughest training regimens in the world. At times, the dropout rate exceeds 90 percent, but on aver-age, it is 75 percent.

SEALs do not come from other parts of the conventional forces; we are recruited directly from the civilian public. A candidate initially spends over a year in a series of formal training environments, including the following:

- 8-week Naval Special Warfare Prep School

- 3-week Orientation

- 21-week Basic Underwater Demolition/SEAL (BUD/S) training (including Hellweek)

- 7-week Parachute Jump School and Survival, Evasion, Resistance, Escape (SERE)

- 19-week SEAL Qualification Training (SQT)

Upon graduation from SQT, a trainee receives the coveted Navy SEAL Trident, which officially designates him as a Navy SEAL. They receive a Special Warfare Operator Naval Rating or, in the case of a commissioned naval officer, the designation Naval Special Warfare (SEAL) Officer.

Navy SEAL Trident

Once a SEAL receives his Trident, he is assigned to a SEAL Team or to a SEAL Delivery Vehicle (SDV) Team. He then begins an 18-month pre-deployment training program consisting of the following:

- 6-month Professional Development (ProDev)— Individual Specialty Training

- 6-month Unit Level Training (ULT)

- 6-month Squadron Integration Training

From there, some SEALs may receive a medical rating through a six-month Special Operations Combat Medic Course. For officers, there's a Junior Officer Training Course for operations planning.

Prescreening the Candidates

As the number one recruiting effort for the Navy since 9/11, we sent retired Navy SEALs all over the country to recruit and mentor candidates. We broke our silence and made commercials, even recruiting movies.

We have never had as many candidates as we did at the height of the wars in Iraq and Afghanistan. We were receiving about 10,000 applications a year and operating beyond full capacity, as we can accept only 1,200 or so a year to start training. Out of 1,200, the most that we have graduated is about 250. The odds of making it through SEAL training are not high.

Trainees who don't make it through not only cost the taxpayers a lot of money but they also slow down the process of growing the organization, which ultimately affects the nation's mission.

We also developed a test called the Computerized Special Operations Resilience Test (C-SORT), delivered alongside an IQ test and a physical test to help us select candidates. The battery of tests doesn't tell us exactly who will make it and who won't— but it does identify the bottom 19 percent of candidates who have, statistics tell us, a 97.5 percent chance of quitting. These tests increase our graduation success rates considerably.

From the Streets—Not from the Ranks

One of the unique differences that separate SEAL Teams from other Special Forces is that we recruit SEALs exclusively from the civilian population. Other Special Forces require their candidates to have served in the conventional forces before they cross over.

Why do we select from the streets? Because we want our recruits to learn our ethos and way of life from the beginning. The only candidates that we take from the Navy Fleet are those who have been to BUD/S training and dropped out but were given a high ethos score while in training.

What About Women?

"How many women are in the SEAL Teams?" The answer, so far, anyway, is none. But in the future, I foresee women being more involved in the Naval Special Warfare arena and as leaders within the SEAL community. The essence of leadership has no gender, but throughout the book, I will use the male pronoun as thus far, all of my examples happen to be men.

It's important to note that in the brotherhood of warriors one's color or religion does not matter. All SEALs are created equal from beginning to end, top to bottom.

Training: Up Close and Personal

Once a candidate gets his SEAL contract, he goes to the SEAL Boot Camp in Great Lakes, Illinois. Unlike other branches of the Special Forces, he participates in Boot Camp with *all* the other early candidates for BUD/S training; the process of creating "brotherhood" and "teamability" starts from the very beginning.

After the initial Boot Camp, they stay at Great Lakes to do what we now call the Prep for eight weeks, essentially to prepare for the mental and physical stress of BUD/S training. From the moment they sign their contracts, candidates are taught our ethos and sworn to live it. It comes up repeatedly throughout training.

In over Their Heads: Basic Underwater Demolition/SEAL Training

During Prep, activities and topics are approached using motivational techniques, encouragement, and even kindness. When the core Basic Underwater Demolition/SEAL (BUD/S) training begins, the approach changes considerably!

BUD/S training has three phases and has now been shortened to 21 weeks (it used to be 26 weeks). Our 2½ year pipeline to make a SEAL had a few overlapping components, so we trimmed 5 weeks off the program.

BUD/S training is sacred to every SEAL and one of the most memorable times in our lives. We know our BUD/S class numbers as well as our Social Security numbers or birthdays. We can expose a fake SEAL just by asking a few questions relating to his class number, the timing of his training, and with whom he trained.

First Phase: Selection

This first phase is heavy on selecting and qualifying recruits based on physical and mental strength, and it is relatively light on specific skills training. We might as well call it the "sandy phase" because our candidates are covered in sand for a good bit of this initial seven-week period. Throughout the exercises, and especially when they make mistakes, students "hit the surf" of the Pacific Ocean. The ocean temperature ranges from the low 50s to the low 60s in this area. Once in the water, they roll around in their fatigues to get fully sandy; we call the result a "sugar cookie." They stay sandy until nature dries them or until they hit the surf again. They run six miles a day just to eat. They need to be efficient and fast even when exhausted; there is no excuse for failure.

This phase tests mental toughness and accountability, and it builds a foundation for teamwork and teamability by requiring them to always have a "swim buddy." A swim buddy is a partner with whom to interchangeably lead, follow, and collaborate to get through a situation. It is during this phase that the First, Fast, Fearless ability is tested, and where that mindset really begins to take shape. We test their fears, their endurance, and their commitment.

Hellweek

In the middle of the first phase comes Hellweek, during which, from Sunday to Friday late afternoon, the students never stop active training. They are wet 24/7, their bodies are chafed all over from the sand, their calves are swollen as big as their thighs, and the tops of their scalps have a baseball-sized open sore from carrying a 200-pound rubber boat on their heads. If they are lucky, they will get a total of four hours of sleep a night for the duration of the week, and all of it while they are wet and sandy on the beach. This is a test of will and fortitude; it often breaks some of the toughest men. SEALs view Hellweek with reverence; it is a very intimate and telling time for all SEALs.

Every SEAL I know was disappointed when leadership pressures from the Department of Defense allowed the Discovery channel to film all the training shortly before the 9/11 attacks. The training is not secret, but it is very intimate and "company confidential." In my opinion, to preserve the intensity, effectiveness, and value of this training, only those who go through Hellweek should ever see it. Like a special proprietary technology or even the Coke recipe, its exclusivity helps to define—and preserve—its value.

In this training phase, three shifts of instructors work eight hours at a time. We set it up so the "meanest" instructors work the 4 p.m. to midnight shift because they have the sunset during their shift. Sunset is dreaded by students because it marks the beginning of what they know will be a long cold night. We watch for the green flash of the sunset, and then yell for them to hit the surf. I shiver just thinking about it.

By the time we "secure the class" on Friday, they will have run over 200 miles with that 200-pound boat either on their heads or in their hands at low carry, in soft sand nearly the entire time. God only knows how many pushups, bear crawls, and other physical tasks they have done! At the end of the session, all instructors and staff line up to shake the hands of the ones who've succeeded, and they say with a smile: "Congratulations, now you only have 17 weeks left of this training!" Admittedly, it's a little sadistic, but it's meant to reinforce our way of life upon them. As we SEALs like to say, "The only easy day was yesterday."

Second and Third Phases: Total Immersion

After students complete three more weeks of the first phase after Hellweek, the program becomes more technical during the second phase of BUD/S training, during which the candidates prepare to become waterborne specialists. Starting with pool comp (competency), they become expert combat divers. Long days and nights in and under the water make this phase tough but in a way that is different from the first phase. It moves more toward actual training than pure selection based on physical and academic strength, but clearly some selection still goes on here as it does through the remainder of the training program.

During the last seven weeks of BUD/S training, we finally get into weapons and explosives training. Most of it is conducted off the coast of California's San Clemente Island, a place where "nobody can hear you scream." During this phase, students again might get four hours of sleep per night while having to learn a considerable amount of technical information.

After Hellweek, it is almost unheard of for a student to quit. When thinking of intense military training programs, people often imagine stereotypical sergeants yelling and screaming at the recruits all the time. We don't do it that much. We build the training program conditions—hard as hell, cold, wet, and miserable—and let the program do the work. They know what they have to do; they have tests and milestones to meet. It's really a form of quality control.

By the second and third phases, most instructors no longer have to raise their voices. They often smile while they teach. "Hit the surf" is just a matter-of-fact command, nothing else. Our leaders lead by example—"power by example, not examples of power"—and they create leaders in the process.

Parachute Jump School

After SEAL candidates graduate from BUD/S training, they learn static line and freefall parachute skills. *Static line jumping* is an old and relatively straightforward activity: they hook a cord to a cable inside the airplane and jump out the door, as you've seen in old World War II movies of the invasion of Normandy.

Freefall jumping takes more time: they are required to jump from 30,000 feet, with oxygen, carrying upward of 150 pounds of equipment, at night.

Then they do Survival, Evasion, Resistance, Escape (SERE) training, which teaches them how to evade capture if caught behind enemy lines and how to resist while captive in various scenarios. Of course, because our enemies often behead their captives, you don't get caught in the first place! That's the first and most important lesson.

SEAL Qualification Training

SEAL Qualification Training (SQT) is 19 weeks long and further enhances the water and land skills that the candidates have been working on from the beginning of training. Despite the term "qualification training," after BUD/S training, there is no more "hit the surf" or any other physical "remediation" given to the students. It's now all training and not much selecting.

SEAL Qualification Training is all about standards. Everyone who gets qualified has to meet all the standards, or they will get

rolled back into the next class behind them. Just as in BUD/S training, if someone gets hurt or doesn't meet the standard, he gets to
roll back and start over—but only once. If he doesn't make it the
second time, he is deemed unfit to be a SEAL or not trainable.

More Than Just a Symbol: Receiving the Trident

The Trident is the Navy SEAL insignia qualified candidates receive
after 58 weeks of training. We all wear it on our left chest on every
uniform. Each SEAL also receives a classic K-bar knife with the
name of one of our fallen SEAL brothers on it. They become
experts in the history of that fallen SEAL, and they bear his legacy
to the rest of the SEAL Teams.

Pre-Deployment Training

After the 58-week core training is complete, the candidate is
assigned to one of the eight standard SEAL Teams to do another
16 to 18 months of training with that unit before he can deploy
overseas. Finally, after 2½ years of training are completed, candidates are fully qualified and ready to deploy.

Upon returning from a deployment, SEALs begin another
16 to 18 months of training once again. Any SEAL not actively
deployed is in some form of training to hone his skills or to
develop new ones. For instance, SEALs may become experts in
individual skills, such as sniper, explosive breacher, driving, or a
foreign language. By the time they become senior enlisted personnel, they are experts in all forms of warfare and can act as key leaders in each unit.

> **One's training is never complete.**

Shoot, Move, Communicate

Much of our skills training focuses on shooting, diving, jumping, and assaults. Our philosophy: if you can "shoot, move, and communicate," you can accomplish any mission. When we assault a building, we work the flow. It is not a choreographed assault like the assaults you see in the movies. We learn basic principles of fields of fire, 360-degree coverage, and movement, but we don't restrict the assault. When you blow the door of the building at night and go through the "fatal funnel" (the doorway), as we call it, you need to be fluid because you have no idea what you will encounter or how the rooms will be set up.

I could train a bunch of Hollywood types to assault a certain building and, within a few hours, they would look, to the untrained eye, like a high-speed Special Forces unit. But if I went into that building and blocked off a door, a stairwell, or anything else, they would look like Keystone Cops running around aimlessly. They wouldn't have skill sets but rather specific movements that they had been trained to do. They could go with the script, but they wouldn't be as good at going with the flow. In contrast, the SEALs train to the truths of skills and tactics and apply them to the situation.

First, Fast, Fearless as a style of leadership means to prepare but also to adapt and flex with the situation, applying strength without pause for deliberation to solve a problem or move an enterprise forward. *First, Fast, Fearless* as a book is designed to reveal fundamental truths about "action" leadership that can be applied in any leadership environment or context.

From here, we explore the three key facets of leadership in the SEAL world: the Brand of the leader himself, the Brotherhood of SEAL Teams, and the Battle Rhythm with which SEALs conduct our activities and move forward. Parts I, II, and III of this book cover each idea, with relevant lessons for the peacetime world.

TAKEAWAYS

- A warrior seeks to win or defeat, not just to destroy.
  A warrior is a leader.

- Physical and moral courage, teamability, and problem-solving ability are core SEAL traits.

- Descended from World War II Special Operations Teams, SEALs formally came to be in 1962. There are eight regular and two specialized SEAL Teams: 2,700 total personnel, 1,200 of whom are combat ready.

- As candidates, wrestlers and chess players are especially successful.

- Formal training takes 2½ years. Core SEAL training takes 58 weeks, including the 21-week BUD/S training, before assignment to a SEAL Team. Pre-deployment training within that team takes another 18 months.

- We take candidates directly from the streets, not the conventional forces. About 10,000 apply each year; 1,200 are accepted into training; and at most, 250 make it through.

- Our training is never complete.

- Our Trident is our symbol; our ethos is our guide.

- We are all leaders and followers.

PART I

DO YOUR PART FIRST

The Brand of a True Leader

You must be the change you want to see in the world.

—MAHATMA GANDHI

When SEALs load up equipment for a mission, it's done in steps. Loading what's closest to your body is the *first-line step*. These are critical items—"must-haves," not "nice-to-haves"—that you don't discard even when on the run and discarding other pieces of equipment.

Leadership works the same way. A leader must gear up with certain first-line items before expecting anything of others. Leaders must live by the same principles and values that they expect from their teams and people. Leadership is about action: leaders must do their part before asking others to do theirs. Walk the walk; don't just talk.

Great leaders throughout history have understood the importance of living a life of virtue, values, and empathy—traits that must come through consistently in their daily behavior. They see things through the eyes of their people and work with their people—not above them—to get things done. Great leaders develop these traits and behaviors into a *style* that ultimately resonates with their teams. That style, applied consistently, builds trust with their teams and through the greater organization. That style builds trust much the same way a consumer brand signals the consistent quality of a product or service.

That style becomes a leadership *Brand*. Every leader should invest a first-line effort into developing a good one.

CHAPTER 2

What Do I Mean by "Leader"?

A leader ... is like a shepherd. He stays behind the flock, letting the most nimble go out ahead, whereupon the others follow, not realizing that all along they are being directed from behind.

—NELSON MANDELA, *A LONG WALK TO FREEDOM*

For 20 years, I've seen it done right, and I've seen it done wrong. In my active SEAL duty, I've mostly seen it done right.

A good leader gets it done—that is, he or she gets the team moving toward the strategic objective, whatever that might be. A good leader gets the team to follow, effortlessly and painlessly. The team members follow in rhythm, to get the right things done, without constant prodding or course correction.

> When leadership is right,
> you don't see it anymore.

A Definition of *Leadership*

> "Leadership is getting people to want to do,
> and to be able to do, something important."
> —Peter Sander, *What Will Steve Jobs Do?*

The prior definition applies to all forms of leadership, whether in a high-tech company, a special military operation, or a charity fund drive. We strive every day to make people want to achieve the objective, to do it willingly, and to *be able*—that is, to have the resources, training, and empowerment—to do it. And what is it we're trying to do? Something important.

One way to bring this definition home is to revert to the game of "opposites" we might have played as kids. As a leader, (1) if your people don't want to perform, (2) if they aren't able to perform, and/or (3) if the task you are trying to perform isn't important, then you fail.

Allow me to share the *five pillars of leadership*—the elements of leadership that keep it strong and move any organization forward. These pillars come directly from the pen and from the experience of Admiral James B. Stockdale, a U.S. Navy Vice Admiral and one of the most highly decorated officers in history.

The Five Pillars of Leadership

Admiral Stockdale was born on December 23, 1923, in Abingdon, Illinois. After graduating from the Naval Academy in 1946, he attended flight training in Pensacola, Florida, and in 1954, was accepted to the Navy Test Pilot School where he quickly became a standout and served as an instructor for a brief time....

In August 1964, Stockdale played a key role in the Gulf of Tonkin incident, which the Johnson administration used to justify large-scale military action in Vietnam. Stockdale always maintained that he had not seen enemy vessels during the event, but on the next morning, August 6, 1964, he was ordered to lead the first raid of the war on North Vietnamese oil refineries.

On September 9, 1965, at the age of 40, Stockdale, who was the Commanding Officer, was catapulted from the deck of the USS *Oriskany* for what would be the final mission. While returning from the target area, his A-4 Skyhawk was hit by antiaircraft fire. Stockdale ejected, breaking a bone in his back. Upon landing in a small village, he badly dislocated his knee, which subsequently went untreated and eventually left him with a fused knee joint and a very distinctive gait.

Stockdale wound up in Hoa Lo Prison, the infamous "Hanoi Hilton," where he spent the next seven years as the highest-ranking naval officer and leader of American resistance against Vietnamese attempts to use prisoners for propaganda purposes. Despite being kept in solitary confinement for four years, in leg irons for two years, physically tortured more than 15 times, denied medical care and malnourished, Stockdale organized a system of communication and developed a cohesive set of rules governing prisoner behavior. Codified in the acronym BACK US [BACK is a rather deep acronym meaning, "Don't **B**ow in public, stay off the **A**ir, admit no **C**rimes, and never **K**iss them goodbye; while US stands for "**U**nity over **S**elf"], these rules gave prisoners a sense of hope and empowerment. Many of the prisoners credited these rules as giving them the strength to endure their lengthy ordeal. Drawing largely from principles of stoic philosophy, notably Epictetus' *The Enchiridion*, Stockdale's courage and decisive leadership was an inspiration to POWs and to military personnel everywhere.

The climax of the struggle of wills between the American POWs and their captors came in the spring of 1969. Told he was to be taken "downtown" and paraded in front of foreign journalists, Stockdale slashed his scalp with a razor and beat himself in the face with a wooden stool, knowing that his captors would not display a prisoner who was disfigured. Later, after discovering that some prisoners had died during torture, he slashed his wrists to demonstrate to his captors that he preferred death to submission. This act so convinced the Vietnamese of his determination to die rather than to cooperate that the Communists ceased the torture of American prisoners and gradually improved their treatment of POWs. Upon his release from prison in 1973, Stockdale's extraordinary heroism became widely known, and he was awarded the Medal of Honor by President Gerald Ford in 1976. (*Source*: U.S. Naval Academy [USNA], Stockdale Center for Ethical Leadership, "Vice Admiral James B. Stockdale," biography, www.usna.edu/ethics)

In the story of Admiral Stockdale, you see the importance of having a code to live by. The military has a simple and specific code of conduct in the event that an American soldier is captured and becomes a prisoner of war. The code gives the framework for a prisoner to resist with honor.

During his captivity, Admiral Stockdale identified the five pillars of "combat leadership," a special kind of leadership in times of what we later coined VUCA (volatility, uncertainty, complexity, and ambiguity). These five pillars of leadership are the leader as a *moralist, jurist, teacher, steward,* and *philosopher.*

Leader as Moralist

In the SEAL world, we talk about leaders staying on the high ground and never losing ground. The idea originates in warfare, as each side's army tries to capture the superior fighting position, which is the highest elevated land. It is exponentially more difficult to fight an enemy uphill from you to whom you are exposed. This battle principle becomes a useful metaphor for moral substance, which we constantly enforce with leaders from the time they enter training.

Upholding a strong sense of values and having respect requires leaders to fight for that moral high ground and to hold it at all cost. Those values, which will be explored throughout the book, are stated most simply in our ethos.

With morals and values, as in physical combat, it is difficult to get back up the hill once you have fallen. People can make mistakes, and everyone understands that, but mistakes in applying values are extremely difficult, and sometimes impossible, to overcome. Lying, cheating, stealing, and other self-serving mistakes make it difficult for followers to respect and trust you—ever.

At the end of the day, it's all about trust. As Warren Buffett once said, "It takes 20 years to build a reputation and five minutes to ruin it. If you think about that, you'll do things differently." Buffett offers another pearl of wisdom about trust and reputation, equally part of the SEAL playbook and mine as well: "Trust is like the air we breathe. When it's present, nobody really notices. When it's absent, everybody notices."

While it's easy for many of us to align ourselves behind these wisdoms, I should point out that this principle applies to actions both big and small. For example, when leaders take credit for the work of others, it is akin to stealing, and the ones they steal it from know it. Hypocritical leaders who set policies and standards but fail to adhere to them are cheating and lying. Furthermore, those who don't have the courage to tell their boss the truth are violating trust. Trust is a two-way street: it is vital for leadership at all levels to set the conditions so that their subordinates *are able to* do the right thing.

It's important to make the distinction between the rule of law and morality. What is legal isn't necessarily what is moral. Moral leadership is *doing the right thing*, not just "doing things right."

Leader as Jurist

A member of a jury doesn't always get all the information available about a case. Sometimes the information is contradictory; eyewitnesses and experts often say opposing things about the same subject. In a trial, the stakes are always high. But in the end, a jurist is compelled to act upon the information given and to render a verdict. It's not a perfect system, but the system relies on people making the best decision they can with the information available. The system, in fact, relies on jurists who have no personal vested interest other than fairness—and ultimately justice.

Similarly, leaders of all stripes often must make decisions that aren't black and white and that aren't based on complete information. In the world of VUCA, decisions are *hardly ever* black and white; they are always a shade of gray. The right answer isn't definite or clear, nor is the wrong answer.

Yet leaders must act and be decisive when it's time to do so. Their decisions affect the outcomes of their organizations and the lives of their people. Their decisions are personal. In fact, it's far from the truth when people say that "it's not personal" when referring to a hard decision they had to make. Of course it was personal.

Leader as Teacher

In the SEAL Teams, every leader at all levels is expected to pass on knowledge and guide and mentor his subordinates. We train our subordinates to do our job and to be ready for the next step. In practical terms we do this to make no single person irreplaceable. In war you must be ready for your number two man to take over in case you go down. Obviously, this metaphor is less drastic in a typical enterprise environment, but the guiding principle still holds: if you get taken out of the picture, the team will continue to carry out the mission. No organization is safe if one person in the chain of command is irreplaceable.

Good leaders train their subordinates (and others on adjacent teams) to take over when they're not there, whether they're gone for five minutes or permanently. Leaders as teachers have clearly defined goals with high expectations for their people, and they help guide them to attain those goals. Coaching is what great teachers do. They don't always give you the answer; they help guide you to find the answer yourself.

Good teachers care about their people and give them some of the most precious commodities they have: their time and attention. Making time—creating time—for your teams is one of the most valuable things you can do as a leader.

Every great leader that I have worked for has taught me something I still carry with me today. You'll find those lessons throughout this book.

Leader as Steward

Leadership is a great privilege and a great responsibility, not just to the organization, to your boss, or to yourself but to your people too. A leader is a servant to his or her team.

Five years before the philosopher and advocate Robert Greenleaf published "Essentials of Servant Leadership," his first essay on the topic, Admiral Stockdale had been living a life of servant leadership in the POW camp. Servant leaders are also stewards of the mission, the people, and the position that they hold. They protect what they are responsible for, and they do it with humility and generosity.

Leaders in the SEAL Teams constantly talk about stewardship in everything we do and in every aspect of our job. We know that we are stewards of America's mission and of the taxpayers' money. But we are also stewards of the people in our care. We do a dangerous job, and we have chosen the responsibility for the lives of people's sons, brothers, husbands, and fathers. Stewards love their people and care about their well-being.

Leadership from the Back of the Line

From day one of BUD/S training until you are no longer on active duty as a SEAL, officers and senior enlisted leaders eat last no matter what the setting. In BUD/S training, the officers and enlisted train side by side, but the officers eat last, even after enlisted instructors. There are no segregated cafeterias or parking lots in SEAL land.

(continued)

> Officers eat last because we are stewards and servant leaders. Eating last is a gesture to reinforce to you, as a leader, that your mission and people come first and before you. You may get paid more and enjoy greater prestige, but you are the guardian of your people—you will stand for them, and they will stand for you.

Leader as Philosopher

In the Merriam-Webster dictionary, a *philosopher* is defined as, paraphrasing, a person who studies ideas about knowledge, truth, the nature and meaning of life, and so on. Throughout my time as a SEAL leader and follower, I have believed in the importance of studying things in detail to find the essence and meaning in them. Flexing this mental muscle helps leaders understand abstract and complicated ideas.

That same dictionary defines *philosophical* as, again paraphrasing, having a calm attitude toward a difficult or unpleasant situation. Such a mantra will always serve leaders well in times of VUCA when stress and fear are at their highest. Leaders need to embrace this and understand that if they cannot control themselves during times of difficulty, they cannot expect their subordinates to control themselves either. Ultimately, practicing a philosophical mindset helps leaders find the right course of action during the most difficult times. As a leader, you should be patient, think things through, and assure yourself and others that your actions—or inactions—will be meaningful.

Lessons for the Business World

At the end of the day, being a leader means getting those around you to be able and willing to do something important. As a leader, your primary responsibilities are to set the direction and remove the roadblocks, so that your people can succeed, and that doesn't happen if your people think that what they're doing isn't important or is meaningless—or worse, is stupid.

Leadership requires trust, insight, honesty, integrity, and humility to work in almost any environment. In the SEAL environment, good leadership is critical—without it, missions fail and people are killed. The consequences may not be so dire in the enterprise environment, but if you follow the *leadership* definition and supporting pillars to a tee, you will achieve your objectives—surpass them, really—and leave your people wanting more.

TAKEAWAYS

- Leadership is getting people to want to—and to be able to—do something important.

- The five pillars of leadership hold the leader to be a moralist, jurist, teacher, steward, and philosopher.

- Moral leadership is principled leadership that occasionally transcends the rules. It builds trust by doing the right things, not just doing things right.

- Leaders must be honest and forthright, and they must do the best they can with often limited facts and resources. Decisions and actions are shades of gray, not black and white.

- Leaders must always teach, train, and develop their people to fulfill their responsibilities in their absence and to take their place, if necessary. A leader who must be in the middle of everything is destined to failure.

- Time and attention are among the most valuable resources a leader has—and can give.

- Leaders do best when they act with empathy and humility.

- Leaders must share in thought as well as in action, and they should understand the greater meaning of any action.

- It's a good idea to put into practice the leadership definition and the five pillars of leadership. Be mindful of what happens when any element is missing.

CHAPTER 3

Owning Your State of Mind: The First Strike Mindset

When your opponent is hurrying recklessly, you must act contrarily and keep calm. You must not be influenced by the opponent.
—MIYAMOTO MUSASHI

After 9/11, every SEAL I know was racing to the front to get to Afghanistan. When the attack happened, I was at BUD/S training as the officer in charge of the final phase of training. We were out in the desert training the students in weapons shooting and tactics. In the compound on the top of the hill, we have a kitchen and satellite TV. I walked into a room full of SEALs about a minute before the second plane hit the World Trade Center. We knew that an act of war had just been committed against America. I drove back to the command that day. Everyone was moving and planning. I had arrived at the training command a few months earlier, so most of my old team members were still on the same SEAL Team.

I received permission from my Commanding Officer and the Commanding Officer of my former team to ready my old team to surge forward. That is, until we got word that it wasn't going to happen: we were in for a long war. You can imagine how that made me feel—or can you? It was one of the lowest moments that I can remember.

More than anything, each one of us wanted to be the first at the front. I was so torn up about not being able to go that I took a week of leave and did nothing but watch the news. We wanted to go. Senior military officers came to inform us that it would be a long fight and that we would get our shot at it. Little did we know that we would get more than our share.

SEALs are *first strike thinkers*. We want to be up front. Beyond all else, we are action oriented. We embrace adversity. We channel fear into courage and action. It's what we call the "first strike mindset." It's a central feature of the First, Fast, Fearless leadership Brand.

Miyamoto Musashi, the author of the opening quote, was the greatest swordsman in Japanese history. He spent his life mastering his swordsmanship, but most important, he understood the need to master himself. SEALs understand this and strive every day to be the cause of the effect, not the effect that was caused. Great leaders act with deliberate intent.

> **Be the cause, not the effect.**

The First Step: Turning Fear and VUCA into Courage and Action

In the military, during times of war and insurgencies, leadership has to deal VUCA. This type of environment can easily create fear, uncertainty, and doubt. Even in the most stressful and VUCA times, SEALs take action (First), move with a purpose (Fast), and commit ourselves and become fully engaged (Fearless).

Leadership is, first and foremost, a choice and a state of mind. You can and must work to control your state of mind to be an elite leader in any organization. You don't leave things up to chance; you go on the offensive.

Think about how the holiday season can change our state of minds. The condition is set for people to be happy, loving, and peaceful. The rest of the year, when we think about the world, most of us return to a fearful and negative state of mind. Why? Because what we see in the news and elsewhere highlights the negative. Focusing on the negative puts us in a negative and hurtful state of mind.

The same happens in an organizational environment. You worry about the competition. You worry about the boss. You worry about coworkers. You worry about the product. You worry about the market. You worry about the tangle of bureaucracy. Pretty soon, when you consider any idea, process, or action within the enterprise, you do so with fear and negativity.

VUCA creates fear. When people don't know what's coming next, they tend to dwell on the dangers and hazards of what *might* come. That fear leads to loss of morale and, ultimately, to inaction. It starts to debilitate you and distract you from the job at hand. Fear shuts down the creative part of your brain. You miss steps and make mistakes, making the problem worse.

How do you turn fear into courage and courage into action? I can't give you a precise formula that works in every environment, but I've experienced a lot of combat and a lot of touchy leadership situations. It boils down to two main things: the first is creating a positive, look-forward environment called a *front sight focus*; and the second, and closely related to the first, is adopting a *first strike mindset*.

Front Sight Focus

People naturally deal with fear in several ways. One that I see repeatedly is the tendency for people to think negatively and "lock up" emotionally and physically; another is the tendency to look for support and companionship to get them through. Unaided, the fearful individual can simply shut down, certainly in the face of combat, and often in the face of required action in an enterprise.

As a leader, one of the most important tasks is simply to be there and to create a positive environment. Leaders present in times of stress are far more valued than those who stop by once in a while when things are going well.

Just being there, however, won't suffice. The next task is to keep the troops moving forward, letting them know you're there alongside them. Approach what lies ahead with positivity and ideas on how it can be changed for the better. How you do this will vary according to your situation and context, but if you maintain a front sight focus, it's likely to rub off on your teams.

Public speakers talk about "channeling the butterflies to fly in formation." That phrase is an accurate description of leadership. We are channeling scattered, random, and even negative energy into a "we can do this" mindset.

Creating a positive mindset also comes with a measure of preparation. Make sure you and the team are equipped with the right resources and knowledge of the situation, or else your positive energy can turn negative very quickly. Be there, and model a positive environment for your people.

> Leaders present in times of stress are far more valued than ones who stop by once in a while when things are going well.

First Strike Mindset

Now that your troops are facing forward and "flying in formation," the next step is to adopt a *first strike mindset*. Take the offensive, and lean yourself and your teams toward action.

This all sounds good, but what are we really accomplishing? Aren't we possibly adding some risk to the situation? Perhaps, but accepting some risk is how things get done and how stress and fear and negative energy are overcome. In a nutshell, a first strike mindset helps protect you and your teams from the adverse effects of fear and stress—it helps to protect you from the tentacles of inaction.

With a first strike mindset, people don't feel like victims, even in situations in which others would consider them victims. Every SEAL is a testament to the fact that this mindset can be *learned*.

As a leader, to truly develop your credibility and make it work, you must be there in times of stress to channel the negative energy of fear into the positive energy of courage and, ultimately, into action. Embrace the adversity yourself, and deploy a go-forward approach. Action is the antidote to stress and fear.

> **A first strike mindset is the path to action.**
> **Action is the antidote to stress and fear.**

Adopting a First Strike Mindset

For SEALs, a first strike mindset is both an attitude we take in training and an approach to planning, problem solving, and leading our teams. It means that at every moment, in every situation, you act first decisively and assertively to make the most of your time. You approach life and every task in a creative, energetic, positive way.

The fundamental advantage of the first strike mindset is that it puts you in control of every moment in your life. It means that you see every moment of your life—and every leadership moment—as an *opportunity*. Even when life hands you something you didn't plan for, you control *your reaction*, even the terms of engagement with the situation. Your life becomes your own when you adopt a first strike mindset and make a habit of using it.

In BUD/S training, we occasionally bring a full staff to the students and "hammer" them for extended periods of time. We make them run up soft sand berms and do buddy carries, sprints, and an assortment of physical exercises. We can see the students start to feel sorry for themselves and wonder why this is happening. We call it the "RAW deal" (RAW, which is war spelled backwards, stands for "random ass whipping"). For elite leaders this is a critical point in mental toughness. We understand that sometimes bad things happen. We may not deserve it, or it may not be fair, but we have to acknowledge it and move on.

Doing tough things, doing them together, and staying positive through it all while thinking, acting, and reacting to all possibilities as they happen will get you a long way. The point here is to make things happen, not to let them happen to you—*to be the cause, not the effect.*

Illustrating the First Strike Mindset

During martial arts training, we use the following scenarios and others like it to illustrate the first strike principle:

> Imagine you're in a parking garage late at night. You're tired. You think you're alone as you arrive at your car and reach into your pocket for your keys. Suddenly, from out of nowhere, a large man moves toward you and reaches for you. It is clear that he means to do you harm.
>
> At this moment, as in every moment of your life, you have a fundamental choice to make about how you will respond. Life has thrust this situation upon you, and there will be an outcome, one way or another. And the way you react, as in every moment of your life, will determine that outcome. Fight, flight, or freeze? You will be the cause or the effect of what happens in the next moment.
>
> If you are standing in this garage late at night and this thug comes at you, and your immediate response is to

defend yourself against this attacker or to block his attempt to grab you, then he has momentum on his side. You have made yourself the "victim" and this guy the "attacker." We always say, "Don't fight unless you have to, but when you do have to fight, fight like you picked it."

But if, instead, you think of striking this guy, exploiting his stupidity, finding a way to make him sorry he dared get close to you, and making sure he never attacks anyone else, then you will view the situation in an entirely different way. You make the rules. In that one moment, before you have even moved a muscle, you have already made yourself the attacker and the defender. Your first move, whatever it is, will be imbued with your sense of direction and purpose. This guy is nothing more to you in this moment than any other obstacle that you have overcome in life.

It is widely understood by psychologists and career professionals that control over your circumstances is at the heart of mental health, productivity, and even happiness. When you're in control of your life, you are happier. What I am saying here—and what all SEALs know—is that you can train yourself to exert control in any situation. You can become the motivation for your own actions. You can act in ways that you, and not your environment, determine are right. You can, in a word, *power* the events in your life and your attitude toward them.

Playing Offense, Not Defense

Offensive thinkers don't dwell on their pain or the unfairness in their lives. They are never victims, or even "survivors," a word that is often synonymous with "victim." They simply never think of themselves in this way.

It's not a matter of seeing a glass as half empty or half full. It's about your control over how you see a fundamental unfairness in your life. Life will surely seem unfair to you at times, but it will seem unfair to everybody at times. To label yourself, or even to think of yourself, as a "victim" of this unfairness is to accept a defensive stance in your life.

> **Offensive thinkers don't dwell on their pain or the unfairness in their lives.**

The lesson SEALs learn during BUD/S training, and continue to learn throughout our careers and later lives, is that it's a choice that is fully in your control:

Iraq War, summer of 2004. The war had become an insurgency that summer. We didn't have a clue what the environment was like or what the real situation was in the streets. We had all seen the public beheadings done by the Al Qaeda–linked Abu Masab al-Zarqawi. I remember seeing the video of a kid traveling in Iraq who had been abducted by al-Zarqawi and his brethren. They put him in the infamous orange jumpsuit and beheaded him on television for all to see. I decided there was no way I would ever be in that situation.

So before I went to Baghdad, I planned what I would do if I became stranded in the middle of the city with no communications with our forces and no response force to rescue me. I had to take every step I could to prepare to control that situation. I tweaked all my gear for a firefight in the cheap little car I would be driving, and I rehearsed every part of the firefight in advance. I practiced shooting through real car windows, and I rammed my car into other vehicles so that I would know how it would react and how I would reach my weapons after a crash.

When I showed up in Baghdad, I had already gone through everything in my mind and had planned it to the letter. I had loaded enough ammunition to melt my barrel more than a few times. I figured that if I died on the streets, my barrel would look like something out of an Elmer Fudd cartoon, bent and smoking hot, from all the ammunition I had put through it. Bullets and bombs are cheap, so I·decided I would be very generous with the enemy when I came in contact with them.

What worried me the most was being captured and having my family and friends watch me on TV, sitting there in an orange jumpsuit like a pathetic wounded animal while the enemy spouted their propaganda before beheading me in victory. That was worse to me than the knowledge that death could be just around the corner.

I taped 30-round magazines and grenades all over the inside of my car, where I could reach and throw them until my arm fell off. I can throw grenades the distance of a mile. But what happens when things go south, and I am pinned down and wounded badly enough to be unable to fight anymore? This was a worry. So I placed two bullets in every pocket of my uniform and equipment, one for my rifle and one for my Sig [Sig Sauer 9 mm pistol]. I must have stashed 8 or 10 pairs of bullets all over me. I figured if I were wounded, I could still get to one of the pockets.

If I were to find myself in this situation, this last bullet would be my "last meal." I rehearsed breach loading both my rifle and my pistol and putting each in my mouth, like you rehearse all good tactics—so that muscle memory would take over and it would be quick. This may sound horrible to most—it does to me now—but it gave me comfort, knowing that I would control what happened to me. I would not allow the enemy to kill me on television and drag me through the streets in that orange jumpsuit. Knowing that I could control my fate gave me peace of mind.

VUCA? Stress? Hell, yes.

I got through this, in part, by adopting a first strike mindset and, in particular, through preparation. I channeled the butterflies. Now I know you don't face situations *this* stressful in corporate America! Your life isn't on the line—although it may seem that way at times. But the same process applies: prepare, look forward, and be ready to make the first strike.

Be First, Fast, Fearless.

Perfect Information? Not!

One advantage that the first strike mindset will give you: you will never be paralyzed by a lack of information. Any leader who deals in VUCA understands that sometimes there simply is no right answer, at least not a perfect one. And yet elite leaders are largely defined by how well they can function with less information than they should have or would like to have. That said, they do well when there's too much information too.

Uncertainly is a fact of life. Successful leaders who adopt a first strike mindset can function at a higher level, despite the fear of everyone around them. The ability to react to situations you did not create, and in which you are outnumbered or disadvantaged in some way, is a hallmark of leaders—and of heroes. SEALs face the most uncertain scenarios known to humanity, and our lives are often on the line. But our first strike mindset makes every situation an opportunity to solve a problem, to face a challenge—and to get it right.

Will You Always Win? Probably Not.

The first strike mindset helps protect you from the adverse effects of stress. Defensive people and those who see themselves as victims are drained by stressful situations. They dread these situations and suffer through them. But people who have a first strike mindset are different. They don't feel like victims, even in situations in which other people would consider them such. This does not mean that you will win every situation because, frankly, sometimes the odds are so stacked against you that you cannot. And certainly a Navy SEAL has the advantage over a mugger in a parking garage because the SEAL happens to be a trained fighter.

But that's not the point. The point is that every move you make is on your terms, and whatever life gives you, you will make it work to your advantage, or at least make it play out in terms that you control. It means that you are not a victim. It does not mean that you lie to yourself or delude yourself. SEALs have learned that you create the reality that plays out in your life, and you do it by adopting a first strike mindset in every moment of your life.

It is the mindset of a First, Fast, Fearless leader.

TAKEAWAYS

- VUCA is volatility, uncertainty, complexity, and ambiguity. Our world and your world are both full of it.

- VUCA causes fear, and fear causes inaction.

- When people don't know what's coming next, they tend to dwell on the dangers and hazards of what might happen.

- A front sight focus and first strike mindset will overcome fear and VUCA.

- Having a *front sight focus* means being there, being prepared, looking forward, and thinking in positive terms.

- Having a *first strike mindset* means taking the initiative, thinking in action terms, and acting first.

- A first strike mindset will channel fear and adversity into courage and action.

- As a leader, be there in times of stress and adversity. Don't just "stop by."

- Never dwell on pain or unfairness. Deal with challenges head on.

- A first strike mindset overcomes the lack of (or overabundance of) information.

- Be the cause, not the effect.

CHAPTER 4

Power by Example:
The Importance of Ethos

Those who have a "why" to live, can bear with almost any "how."
—FRIEDRICH NIETZSCHE

In 1776 the Declaration of Independence, one of the most important documents in American history and to democracy, was crafted. The words in that document set in motion a process that a mere 240 years later finds America as the world's only superpower:

> We hold these truths to be self-evident, that all men are created equal, that they are endowed by their Creator with certain unalienable Rights, that among these are Life, Liberty and the pursuit of Happiness.

Why is the Declaration of Independence so important? Why has it worked so well, and why has it stood the test of time and change? What is it about the document and its message that has guided us so well?

It's not just a document, and it's not just a set of rules. For American society and culture, it represents an *ethos* guiding our everyday activity and, really, our very being as individuals and as a nation.

What Is an Ethos?

According to the Merriam-Webster dictionary, an *ethos* is, para-phrasing, the distinguishing character, sentiment, moral nature, or guiding beliefs of a person, group, or institution. The word *ethos* means "character" in Greek.

Having an ethos and a code by and for which to live has been around since recorded time. Warriors like the Knights Templar, the samurai, and the Spartans for whom SEALs and other U.S Special Forces have a particular affinity all lived by a code.

The code not only guides behavior but it also becomes part of the "brand" of the group or team. The modern combat uniform is designed with Velcro so that rank and insignias can be put on and taken off the uniform easily. It's not uncommon to see a patch with the image of a Spartan on the sleeve of a SEAL unit.

In fundamental ways, the SEAL Ethos and way of life are very similar to those of ancient warriors. True warriors have always held similar fundamental beliefs in the virtues of life. We all believe in serving something greater than ourselves, which gives us a clear purpose and meaning in life. We believe in protecting those who cannot protect themselves and in living a life of virtue, purpose, and brotherhood.

The SEAL Ethos is a highly evolved statement of a shared set of core values, values that guide the thoughts, behaviors, morals, beliefs, and sentiments of SEALs and SEAL Teams. Our ethos is much more than a lofty set of ideas hanging on the walls inside our buildings. It's the basis for all of our conduct on and off the battlefield. It's a philosophy of how to live life as SEALs, citizens, and leaders.

Our ethos is a guiding framework for life and a guiding framework for leadership. It is a central part of the SEAL leadership Brand.

> **An ethos is *your* Declaration of Independence.**
> **It is your guiding light.**

Without Ethos, Chaos?

A few years ago, I helped facilitate a leadership seminar for people from different companies from around the country. I wanted to know whether they had a mission statement at their workplace. Each one of them did. My next question was a little more difficult: I asked them, "Who can quote your mission statement or tell me what it says? If you can, please raise your hand." Out of the 20 or so, one person raised her hand. She actually couldn't tell me her mission statement verbatim, but she did express the spirit of it, so I thought that counted.

Most of those companies had spent a lot of time and money developing mission statements. Days of effort, expensive off-site meetings, plenty of refreshments. The most likely result was a bunch of dull posters scattered throughout the office, hanging on the wall collecting dust. I'll bet most mission and value statements have had a negligible positive effect on company performance. It's easy to find statistics on how engaged, or disengaged, employees are in the workplace.

As SEALs, our ethos is our way of life. We continuously grade and evaluate ourselves—and are graded by others—within the framework of the values stated and implied in our ethos. It defines who we are.

How the SEAL Ethos Evolved

As SEALs, we knew we couldn't afford to regard ourselves or be regarded as merely the steely-eyed killers of the past. Our missions range from going into close quarters combat with our enemies to engaging tribal leaders and conducting irregular and unconventional warfare around the world. SEALs must be diverse thinkers and problem solvers, and they must be trusted to do the right thing with no intent of personal gain.

We can control ourselves and our emotions. We need to have a learner's mindset and should always be studying and thinking, with more tools in our personal toolbox than ever before. Leadership is more than just bringing down the hammer. We know that we have the physical tools, the military hardware, but we must bring our logic, reason, physical strength, and values to bear on everything we do.

Mythos to Ethos: It Starts with Changing the Culture

As a culture, we have been evolving since our beginnings in World War II. Our indoctrination starts at BUD/S training and carries on throughout the SEAL Team experience. Culture is one of the most difficult things to change. We changed our entire command and deployment structure virtually overnight, but we continue to work on our culture.

Ethos can sometimes evolve from a misguided "mythos" of the past. The "break glass in case of war" mentality doesn't work in modern warfare, nor does it work in modern business. In *The Rogue Warrior*, bestselling Navy SEAL author Richard Marcinko (who was convicted and imprisoned in 1990 for defrauding the government) reinforced the steely-eyed killing machine image we had as an organization in the late 1980s and early 1990s. That book and others have projected an image of SEALs as steroid meatheads drinking, fighting, and being outlaw bikers who show up ready to kill when they get the call. We have been fighting that mythos in our culture ever since.

Once you build a brand image, good or bad, it is hard to change without decisive action. One could look at Ford in the 1970s and 1980s as an example of a company that worked hard to escape its "mythos" of cheap, unsafe cars (for example, Pintos) and its more sterling ethos today as a quality manufacturer of electronically advanced, environmentally friendly automobiles.

> Without an ethos, you might become trapped
> in a mythos.

The mythos/ethos dichotomy plays out over and over again in the business world. A business—or a group or a team within a business—may acquire a mythos over time through outright action (or inaction). Such a mythos can be earned, or it can be built through rumor and general skepticism by customers, employees, and/or the general public. This can happen simply due to a lack of a strong, positive ethos. The best way to defend against this is to play offense—that is, to create a strong ethos and deliver to it.

Crafting the Ethos: Decisive and Deliberate

Like Ford, we knew we had to evolve and strengthen our ethos. As a community, we knew we had to take the offensive mindset and create a culture that would produce the warriors our nation needs. An unwritten culture is strong in any organization, but the great organizations capture their culture and determine it with deliberate action.

Deliberate action involves discussing your ethos, your organizational credo, in detail, and it means writing it down. Statistics tell us that the top 2 percent of executives all write down their goals. But in our view, the act of committing it to paper gives it life. We knew we needed to draft an ethos just as our forefathers knew they needed to draft the Declaration of Independence (and write it down, as they did so well!). We needed to set a standard and create a roadmap. We knew we needed a strong code that we could live by. No bland posters on institutional hallways. It was important to know what we wanted at the outset. As Lewis Carroll said, "If you don't know where you are going, any road will get you there."

In 2005, we held a week-long off-site "ethos conference" on San Clemente Island, off the California coast (it was not a corporate travel boondoggle; San Clemente is where we have one of our major training facilities). At this point, we had been at war for nearly four years, and the incidents off the battlefield were taking more people out of the fight than Al Qaeda. The military is held to a different legal standard under the Uniform Code of Military Justice (UCMJ) than our fellow citizens. When there is an infraction of the UCMJ, we can lose pay and our clearance. During that time period, there were many of these infractions, so we felt a clearer statement of our guiding principles was necessary.

Months before this conference, we had a team assigned to collect input and prepare the format for the conference. Just defining the values that you wish to live by is a process that is difficult yet very rewarding. As an organization, we had to define what being a warrior meant and what being a leader meant—at all times. We had to be clear about our calling and how we would conduct ourselves at all times.

Destroy? Defeat? Or What?

This week-long conference was not easy. But it was very productive and perhaps one of the biggest steps forward for SEALs in years. There were many critical words and phrases discussed at great length; we wanted to be as clear, concise, and accurate as possible.

One of the longest debates on the specific words mentioned in the ethos was over the word *destroy* our enemies versus *defeat* them. A seemingly slight difference, but it was significant in our way of thinking. *Defeat* implies winning by the means necessary to do so, which may well avoid violence, while *destroy* centers on violence and destruction ("the hammer"), which may be the means but is never the end.

The debate was significant because it was a clash of schools of thought about being a SEAL, which is at the heart of the idea of ethos. At day's end, neither word made it into the ethos because we needed something better. We don't just defeat or destroy our enemies. We achieve our mission and the goals established by our country, more of a pragmatic, big-picture, goal-driven approach.

Words matter. Choose them carefully.

Setting the Objectives: What Did We Want to End Up With?

Going into the conference, we had clear objectives to meet, all listed below. The participants in the conference were of various ranks and experiences throughout the SEAL Teams, both officers and enlisted personnel:

SEAL Ethos: Objectives

- Must resonate at all levels of Naval Special Warfare
- Strike a balance between humility and warrior message
- Address key concerns and problems
- Deliver an enduring message like the Gettysburg Address
- Inspire all personnel at all levels
- Capture our heritage and that of the Navy as a whole
- Speak outside the community; be relevant outside the SEAL perimeter
- Reinforce on- and off-duty actions
- Be clear and concise, easy to read
- Apply to all occasions like graduations and funerals
- Act as the standard by which we will be judged and judge others

From there, we identified the values that we needed to express and that would capture what a SEAL warrior and leader truly is. Each value is a clearly visible part of the final ethos:

SEAL Ethos: Values

- Integrity
- Leadership
- Discipline
- Courage
- Innovation
- Loyalty
- Teamwork
- Humility
- Fortitude
- Honor
- Commitment
- Service
- Excellence
- Legacy
- Professionalism

These objectives and values are the basis for the SEAL Ethos, our guiding light and set of principles.

Implementing the Ethos

It was one thing to put some ideas down on paper; it was another to get them to resonate and be fully adopted by the SEAL organization and recognized by those outside. This is where many a corporate mission, objective, and ethos-setting session has failed as well.

To be successful, we knew we had to begin with recruiting, which included setting expectations from our first contact with applicants. We decided that when new recruits received a contract, we would present the ethos up front. New recruits know what is expected of them from the day they arrive until the day they leave. They know that if they cannot or do not desire to live up to the ethos, they will not be a Navy SEAL.

Beyond introducing the ethos at recruiting time, we knew we needed to bring it to the BUD/S training staff. The training staff would be the first point of contact, and thus the first impression of the SEAL way. We mandated that instructors live by this code every day. We feathered in principles from our ethos into every training event.

In training, one way we inoculate new candidates with the ethos is by telling "sea stories." Sea stories are meant to be a little peek behind the curtain and to inspire the candidates for the future. The stories show the transition from the "in case of war break glass" mentality to an existence founded on our ethos.

Bringing a First, Fast, Fearless Mindset to Creating an Ethos

Dealing with the sorts of change one might encounter when defining an ethos or, in our most recent case, changing one, can be very challenging. Change of this magnitude won't stick unless you do it with a First, Fast, Fearless mentality.

It all begins with taking the initiative to do the hard thing. Any change of this magnitude needs to be done quickly or it will die on the vine. The ethos must be crafted quickly, and then disseminated quickly to stick and become part of the organization's way of thinking. It takes strong leadership and followership to make such a change stick. Leader as philosopher, as defined by Admiral Stockdale, hits its stride when you work on and by an ethos.

A Code of Honor, Courage, and Commitment

We discussed the meaning of honor and how important it is for us as SEALs and as warrior combatants. We also discussed our enemy's own culture and code of honor. It's not our code, but they consider it their way of being honorable.

We talked about courage and how important both physical and moral courage is to us in our profession. As for our enemy, trust me, they have courage to come out and fight a force that is smarter, better trained, better equipped, and better supported. They have courage as well.

When we discussed the importance of commitment, one of the first things I mentioned was that for years, the enemy had lived in caves in the cold snowy mountains of Afghanistan.

So what is the value that sets us apart from the enemy that we so much want to defeat? I'll illustrate the value with a sea story:

> In Iraq, we were hunting what we call an HVT [high value target], a high-ranking terrorist. I had sent multiple sniper teams out into the city to PID [positively identify] the terrorist, so that we could dispatch a direct action team to get this guy. The Rules of Engagement on an HVT are more lenient than those for lower-level terrorists. To have the authority to shoot someone, that person must first display a hostile act or have hostile intent. An HVT is considered hostile merely by being who he is.
>
> The sniper team that first spotted the HVT was able to get a very clear digital picture of him and send it back via a satellite radio to the TOC [Tactical Operations Center], where I was. I had a picture of the HVT, a recent close-up, taken by a source [spy]. I immediately compared the photo with the one I had already, and I assembled

several members of the team to get their opinion. We had 100 percent agreement that this was our guy. Knowing that people of the same ethnic background can more easily identify features of people of their own kind, I shared the photos with my Iraqi counterparts. They all confirmed that these photos were of the same man. I gave our sniper the green light to kill the HVT if he tried to evade or leave before we could get there. But one person, and the only person, who wasn't convinced that this was our man was our sniper. He had doubts about the identity of the HVT. Being the team leader, he came up with a hasty alternative, in case the man tried to leave before we could roll down to his location.

The man walked out of the house and toward his car. The city we were in during this part of the war was extremely hostile and dangerous for any westerner outside of the fortified compounds. Instead of killing this man, the team sprinted 100 yards in broad daylight into a busy market area and tackled the HVT while our sniper fired high-caliber rounds from a suppressed rifle into the vehicle's engine. This not only kept the car from functioning but it also confused the HVT when he heard sharp cracks going into his car.

The small teams tackled the HVT before he knew what was happening and dragged him into a building and waited until a QRF [Quick Reactionary Force] came to support them.

The moral of the story: our sniper was a true warrior and lived knowing life as a value. He did not kill someone he didn't have to. It turned out he was right: we performed DNA tests using samples taken from the man, and they did not match those of the HVT. In war, frequently, nobody will know what really happened except the person with boots on the ground. Ethos matters.

SEALs know that we don't decide if the enemy lives or dies; it's up to him. If we go into a building and a terrorist puts up his hands, we take him in. If we go in and he puts his hands down on his weapon, we take him out.

The core value that separates us from our enemy is life—a life of liberty and the pursuit of happiness. Our enemy does not respect life nor do they believe that people should be free and happy, at least in the same way we do. Anyone who believes in democracy believes in life as a value—these beliefs are inseparable.

Our ethos, again, provides the guiding light.

Ethos and Daily Conduct

Religions around the world have given people a context by which to live their lives. Ethos-driven people have a clear direction on how to conduct themselves in every aspect of their lives. We often say that the whole man goes to war, so we understand that we must address all parts.

Leadership is no different. You cannot separate business from respect of and care for your employees if you believe in life as a value. Having a strong ethos and code of conduct can transform organizations and change people's lives to ones of purpose and meaning, while exceeding the goals of the organization.

> **Having a strong ethos can transform organizations and change people's lives.**

Deconstructing the SEAL Ethos—and Constructing One of Your Own

I kicked off Chapter 1 by sharing our ethos. I did that not just to lead the conversation about what SEALs are and what we do but also to show right out of the starting gates how powerful a well-crafted ethos can really be. Didn't that ethos stir you, as it does us?

I'll deconstruct our ethos to help you construct your own:

> In times of war or uncertainty there is a special breed of warrior ready to answer our Nation's call. A common man with uncommon desire to succeed. Forged by adversity, he stands alongside America's finest special operations forces to serve his country, the American people, and protect their way of life. I am that man.

That first part describes who we are and distinguishes us as special, determined in service in adversity, a special breed, a breed apart.

How do you define yourself? Your team? What is your role? What are you supposed to accomplish? What makes you special? What sets you apart? Why should others respect you? How do you *earn* that respect?

Try not to get caught up in too much of the business buzz-word game—"best in class," "leading edge," "best practices." Make sure your distinguishing features are really clear and are those that are tangibly different from the crowd.

> My Trident is a symbol of honor and heritage. Bestowed upon me by the heroes that have gone before, it embodies the trust of those I have sworn to protect. By wearing the Trident I accept the responsibility of my chosen profession and way of life. It is a privilege that I must earn every day. My loyalty to Country and Team is beyond reproach. I humbly serve as a guardian to my fellow Americans always ready to defend those who are unable to defend themselves. I do not advertise the nature of my work, nor seek recognition for my actions. I voluntarily accept the inherent hazards of my profession, placing the welfare and security of others before my own. I serve with honor on and off the battlefield. The ability to control my emotions and my actions, regardless of circumstance, sets me apart from other men. Uncompromising

integrity is my standard. My character and honor are steadfast. My word is my bond.

That section is about our heritage and history, why we
exist. The notes of humility and avoidance of personal glory show
through here. Really, that part describes the *personality* of the team
and where it comes from.

What are the special responsibilities and duties provided by
your business or your team? Why are you important? How do you
operate on a daily basis? How do you perceive your people, your
customers, your competition, the "enemy"? What defines, and
guides, your success? What kind of example do you or your team
set for others? How do you want others to perceive you?

> We expect to lead and be led. In the absence of orders I will
> take charge, lead my teammates and accomplish the mission.
> I lead by example in all situations. I will never quit. I perse-
> vere and thrive on adversity. My Nation expects me to be
> physically harder and mentally stronger than my enemies. If
> knocked down, I will get back up, every time. I will draw on
> every remaining ounce of strength to protect my teammates
> and to accomplish our mission. I am never out of the fight.

In that section we discuss how we actually perform, in action.
We describe ourselves as leaders in our field, and we define what
that leadership means. We are not just performers; we are leaders.
Your ethos can do the same. Describe what it means to be a leader
in your business or team function, and how you plan to measure
up to that task.

> We demand discipline. We expect innovation. The lives of
> my teammates and the success of our mission depend on
> me—my technical skill, tactical proficiency, and attention
> to detail. My training is never complete. We train for war
> and fight to win. I stand ready to bring the full spectrum of

combat power to bear in order to achieve my mission and the goals established by my country. The execution of my duties will be swift and violent when required yet guided by the very principles that I serve to defend. Brave men have fought and died building the proud tradition and feared reputation that I am bound to uphold. In the worst of conditions, the legacy of my teammates steadies my resolve and silently guides my every deed. I will not fail.

The last part lays out additional expectations and duties of our teams: innovation, contribution beyond execution of daily tasks, citizenship, teamability, team play, and the utmost respect for our reputation. We embrace the guidance and adherence to moral principles and a greater good. We show that you must have the "right end" in mind. Finally, we wrap up with the short but all-inclusive, "I will not fail."

Your ethos won't be exactly like ours. But the important part is to have one, think one, use one, and allow it to not only guide your daily activities but also to inspire you to First, Fast, and Fearless victories in your enterprise.

TAKEAWAYS

- Like the Declaration of Independence, an ethos is both an expression of who you are and a day-to-day guide to thoughts and actions.

- Without an ethos, not only might you be stuck in VUCA but you might also be trapped in an unfortunate or even inaccurate mythos.

- Creating an effective ethos requires a First, Fast, Fearless mindset as well; it should be an inspired, deliberate, and inclusive exercise for your teams.

- An ethos should be written down in muscular prose. Avoid the usual business jargon. Use specifics; be decisive.

- Cover who you are, what you do, how you excel, why you are who you are, how you'll behave, how you'll treat others, and how you expect to earn respect, among other things.

- Make sure your ethos is really part of your team's culture. Make it "internalizable"—and internalize it. Avoid bland mission statements. Make it a centerpiece of who you are.

- Allow the flexibility to adjust your ethos as necessary.

- Continuously measure yourself and your team against your ethos.

CHAPTER 5

Be It Ever So Humble: There Is No Place Like Leadership

B efore 9/11, I read the book *On Killing: The Psychological Cost of Learning to Kill in War and Society* by Lieutenant Colonel Dave Grossman. It has become a standard text, especially in law enforcement circles, and it offers insight into the psychological implications of killing other human beings. Lieutenant Colonel Grossman refers to several studies showing that, throughout history, human beings did not want to kill each other and often never fired their weapons, even in war.

Grossman cites statistics from the *Civil War Collector's Encyclopedia* by F. A. Lord, which tells us that of the 27,574 muskets recovered from the battlefield after the 1863 Battle of Gettysburg, nearly 90 percent (24,000) were loaded, and 12,000 of those were loaded more than once. These were black powder weapons, which had to be reloaded with powder and a bullet each time they had been fired. It's estimated that 95 percent of the time was spent loading and only 5 percent firing the weapon. This means that 95 percent of the weapons should have been empty and only 5 percent loaded.

But the reverse was true: 90 percent were loaded. What do these statistics tell us?

This remained a mystery for the military until Vietnam, where people were trained to fire their weapon consistently in combat. I was intrigued by another finding: the distance from the act of killing mattered—the greater the distance from the act itself, the easier it was to do.

Thus, it's easier for the captain of a Navy ship to send a cruise missile 500 miles away to destroy a building and everyone inside than it is to engage the enemy at point-blank range and carry out the same amount of destruction. Since 9/11, I have heard from civilians who have never been to war express their opinions on what we should do in the Middle East. Many have expressed the desire to "bomb the hell out of them." This is a clear example of how the vast distance between the cause and the effect of a horrific event makes it easy for some to call for the catastrophic destruction of life. Some of the most hawkish people I've ever met have never been to war, nor have they ever been in the military, yet somehow they are willing to wipe others off the face of the earth!

Where am I going with this? How does the theory of killing people relate to leadership? How is it relevant to business at all? In business, sometimes you speak in life-and-death terms, of "destroying the competition," of "going in for the kill," but it is hardly the same thing. So what am I getting at?

I'm talking about the need for humility—the need for a leader to be humble, to be human, and to serve the needs of his or her people first. It's one of the most important aspects of the SEAL leadership Brand.

> **Your work should be your temple—**
> **it's a chance to express your humanity.**

Where Power *Really* Comes From

We defined *leadership* as "getting people to want to, and be able to, do something important." There were two key phrases in that definition: "want to" and "be able to."

How does this link up with the theory of killing? Simply this: your subordinates—your teams—are people. No matter how far away physically they might be, those teams and subordinates need to come first. And if they are first, they'll put you first. If you're distant, abstract, hard-nosed, hard-assed, they'll pick that up. Leadership is about us, about team, about winning—not about I, me, and mine.

> **Eliminate I, me, and mine.**

The concept of distance and killing opened my eyes to the understanding that the distance from the consequences of your decisions creates abstraction in the consequences of the actions. Those who believe we should "bomb the hell out of them" have never seen up close the effects of doing so. When you have experienced the outcome of that decision, it is not so easy to make— nor should it be.

Leadership is the same. If you are not diligent with self-reflection, the privilege of authority, position, and power will make you a self-serving leader who is morally and emotionally calloused, arrogant, ego driven, and, at the end of the day, simply mean. The higher you rise in an organization, the more privileges you have and the farther the distance between you and the effects your decisions have on your people. That brings more illusions of authority— more authority than you really have—especially when it comes to getting people to *want* to do something important.

Throughout this book, I'll repeat this core theme: that the way leaders treat people drives their loyalty, motivation, trust, and, ultimately, their productivity. Self-serving leaders may be successful in the short term, but they will never be truly effective in tapping into the potential of the organization. The higher the fear and stress level, the more hypersensitive people are to leadership, especially bad self-serving leadership.

> The higher you go, the less you know,
> the more you owe.

Power by Example, Not the Other Way Around

Fortune's most recent list of the World's 50 Greatest Leaders wasn't a surprise to me. The list includes Pope Francis, Warren Buffett, General Joe Dunford, and the Dalai Lama. Are these leaders immersed in the trappings of power? Or do they work with their people, with their teams, with outsiders, to get their messages across and to accomplish their goals?

Number 38 on that list is Eric Greitens, a former Navy SEAL, Rhodes scholar, and founder of The Mission Continues, a motivational organization for veterans. I had the pleasure of training and mentoring Greitens when he was going through BUD/S training. These leaders, including Greitens, who was also named one of *Time* magazine's 100 Most Influential People in the World in 2013, share certain ideas and perspectives of being a leader. None of those ideas are about serving themselves or their egos.

They're about power by example, not examples of power.

Always Share the Load: The SEAL Caricature Skit

Throughout the SEAL experience, we emphasize the need for humility. At the end of each phase of BUD/S training, SEAL students do full-on caricature skits of the instructors, with no constraints.

When these skits are performed, the instructors have no authority to order students to hit the surf, nor can they inflict any other form of physical remediation. The students have complete amnesty from the instructors they are about to rip into and make fun of. The skits are funny, like a lot of things we do at BUD/S— but they're not really about being funny. They're about keeping the instructors humble and honest.

BUD/S instructors are like gods to the students, with power and authority over them beyond anything any instructor has ever had. At any moment, an instructor can make a student drop to the ground to do pushups and leave him there for as long as he wishes. He can send the whole class to the surf to get wet and sandy for the smallest infraction. Most experienced instructors deal well with this power, but some of the newer and younger SEAL instructors don't, and they need a humility check. Actually, we all need a humility check in life; some of us just need it a little more than others!

A System of Humility: You Live It, They See It

In some ways, our SEAL students are like prisoners, in the sense that they are living their training 24/7, whereas we instructors go home at night and enjoy our time doing other things. Our students are crafty—and we want them to be. Like prisoners who find the weaknesses in the guards, the students pay attention to every little nuance of every instructor. Just as a caricature artist sees physical traits and magnifies them on canvas, the students see personal traits and exploit them during the skits.

Students go all out, dressing up and building simple props in order to pick on the weakest instructor traits. If an instructor always tells sea stories of himself in combat trying to prove how badass he is, students may have someone do a Rambo act and run around pretending to kill everyone in the audience. If you happen to have put on a few pounds on shore duty, expect an attack there too. If you are a small instructor and act like a bigger-than-life ninja warrior, you will see that in the skit.

The skits go on for an hour or so; everyone shows up for them, including headquarters, if they're around. As a form of 360-degree feedback, the skits are very enlightening to the instructors. In every way, they'll keep you honest and humble.

All that said, some of the instructors don't take it so well! You will hear them say, "That's bullshit. I don't do that, do I?" Skits are also a form of transparency; sometimes we find out about what went on when leaders were not present.

The point of the whole exercise: authority and power can make you believe your own hype and make you arrogant. But you'll reassume a position of humility when a 21-year-old BUD/S student is hammering the hell out of your weak points in front of everyone. Most of what the students pick on are egocentric traits that instructors show as they train the students. If you are a 45-year-old senior enlisted SEAL and can't quite run as fast as you used to, they may poke a little friendly fun at you, but if you are arrogant and instruct them with your ego, it will be brutal.

Skits are a very important part of our training because they reinforce humility to the students, but more important, they reinforce humility and provide feedback to the instructors. What they really enforce is a *system*, the humility of the instructors and a *recognition* of that humility by the students.

The Art of Humility—and What Skits Can Do for You

Some of the best instructor training comes from the student skits. As a warrior and as a leader, it is critical to keep yourself in check constantly and practice humility. Simply put by my friend Ken Blanchard, "Humility is not thinking less of yourself. It's thinking of yourself less."

I'm not saying that every corporate organization should add skits to their regular routine. The point is for leaders to find ways to look at themselves in the mirror to see a reflection of what their troops think of them. If you're doing things right, then you and your people work well as a team, and your humility will not only be noticed but will also provide a conduit for useful feedback and enhance the work itself.

> **Leadership is something you do *with* people, not *to* them.**

Divorce Your Ego

The biggest enemy of humility is our own ego, which is molded by our fears. Fear, of course, helps to keep us alive by restraining us from jumping out of airplanes and perhaps from becoming a Navy SEAL. But fear also creates insecurity, and the antidote to insecurity for most of us is the ego.

The kind of ego that fear produces is not a good state of mind for leadership. People fear all kinds of things: humiliation, not looking smart, not being appreciated, failure. Much of what we call our personality comes from our fears; it is our ego that defends us from our perceived fears.

When children are born, they are carefree and loving, and they aren't self-conscious of their appearance or what people think of them. But as they grow up, their need to be accepted and appreciated by others shapes their personalities. We are all human, and it's perfectly normal, but we need to be aware of our fears and ultimately control our ego as a leader. Once you understand and see your own fears, you can allow yourself to be humble without being humiliated.

People often say that public speaking is one of their biggest fears; it even ranks higher than death for some. Public speaking entails vulnerability; people are afraid that others will see them truly for who they are and won't approve; they are afraid of shame and ultimately rejection. As with experienced speakers, great leaders learn to divorce themselves from their egos.

At the end of the day, you are there to serve your people, not your ego. If your ego requires more strokes than your people, they will see right through it, and no matter how hard you try, they will find fault with you, which will serve only to make you *more* insecure. Avoid the vicious cycle by putting your ego aside and finding excellence, not fault, with your employees.

> **Tell people what they did right.
> It's a humbling experience.**

The Antidote for Fear: Servant Leadership

If fear is what I want to avoid, and fear in my teams is what I want to avoid *as a leader*, what is on the opposite bank of this river that I should swim toward? The answer, and it may sound strange coming from a steely-eyed Navy SEAL, is that the opposite of fear is *love*. Most people think that the opposite of fear is *courage*, but courage is not the absence of fear. It's acting in the face of fear. We are all born with no personal fears; we are all about pure love. Over time, through experience and the growth that emerges from that experience, that love is hidden by fear—and ultimately leads to the formation of our egos as a coping mechanism.

I first learned of the concept of servant leadership in a class taught by Ken Blanchard in the executive leadership program I attended. I had been in the SEAL Teams for about eight years at this point, and although we don't use the term *servant leadership* in the SEAL Teams, we *do* practice it. We train SEALs to put the mission first, your men next, and yourself last. If there is one piece of advice that all leaders have given me over the years, it's this: "Take care of your men, and they will take care of you." Remember, leaders eat last.

Servant leadership means that the team is not about you. Imagine yourself as a stagecoach driver, with the team carrying you along. Without you, they are still a team, but without them you are a pedestrian. President Kennedy encapsulated this concept when he said, "Ask not what your country can do for you. Ask what you can do for your country." This is pure servant leadership, which requires courage that is rooted in humility.

> At the highest level, we are servant leaders. Everything else is just smoke.

Don't Wear Your Emotions on Your Sleeve

On one of my deployments, I had an officer on my team who was very capable, intelligent, mission driven, and hardworking. But during times of extreme stress, he would blow up in anger and insult the people around him. His temper and position became his weapon. I watched him nearly lose everyone's respect for him because he couldn't control his emotions and his actions as our SEAL Ethos demands.

My Senior Enlisted Advisor (SEA) would make excuses for him, saying that "he wears his emotions on his sleeve," that he was a good guy. But he didn't go around wearing sympathy, compassion, and caring on his sleeve. He wore only anger and frustration.

No matter what, leaders with a servant mindset do not abuse their people. I had some very colorful counseling sessions with this officer, and his behavior did change. Another lesson for those of you leading leaders: leaders don't let *their followers* abuse the people in their care.

As leaders, the higher you go, the more important it is to refine your "trade craft," so to speak, and identify your traits that stand out to people. Just as BUD/S students eventually see the traits of the instructors, so do your employees. They know things about you that you probably don't know about yourself. It's the most important information you can get.

When you wear your emotions—those of anger, frustration, short-temperedness—on your sleeve and you become unreasonable, people will either shut down, or worse, go out of their way to avoid you or hide what they're doing. They will also spend most of their time managing perceptions to avoid your tantrums—and leave you ignorant of a situation. In the SEAL world, this can be disastrous; it isn't too healthy for your enterprise either. Make sure your Brand is about care, compassion, and love.

> When people are scared of their leadership, they spend most of their time managing leadership's perception of them.

A Suggestion That Really Works:
A Suggestion Box

Hanging on the wall outside of every SEAL Commanding Officer's office is a wooden box labeled "Suggestion Box," at the top of which is a slit large enough to put a standard envelope through. The box is padlocked; only the Commanding Officer and his Senior Enlisted Advisor have the key. The box is meant to collect anonymous feedback from anyone and everyone at all levels in the command.

To some leaders, this may seem scary. But why would it be scary to know how people see you? When I was at the University of San Diego, a questionnaire was sent to my subordinates and colleagues with questions about my leadership traits. Like a suggestion box, it was anonymous; it gave a 360-degree view of how people saw me as a leader. This was done for all the leaders in my executive program.

When we got the results, most of my classmates—many were senior leaders, including a few CEOs—were shocked at how their people viewed their leadership. Most of them *thought* that they were humble and acted like servant leaders and that they would get rave reviews from their people.

In fact, they were way off the mark. Some were quite upset and—a good sign perhaps—even cried about the results!

As a leader, you are what others think of you. Spare no effort to find out what they really think.

A Simple Piece of Advice: Stop Being You!

I think the suggestion box is an incredibly good and simple tool to help leaders grow. The suggestion box represents that 360-degree evaluation of your leadership and alerts you to any other issue that may be going on. Thanks to my prior experiences with the suggestion box, the feedback I received from the questionnaire matched what I believed my leadership style to be.

Every step you climb up the ladder of leadership, you need to learn and grow. That is hard to do without accurate and timely feedback from your teams, peers, and subordinates.

The suggestion box—or whatever feedback mechanism you put in place—may contain a few surprises. You often find out that you are not leading the way you think you are. You discover what you need to know about your communication, plans, and policies, and what's important to your people. Sometimes the lesson is for you to stop being you.

This really struck home while I was coaching executives. By the time most of them get to where they are, they are convinced that their strengths are good enough and as good as they need to be. They don't think they are the problem. Often, it's not what they need to learn as much as it is that they need to stop being themselves. During coaching, it's common to hear people say, "That's just who I am," which is one of many ways they have to support—and love—their egos.

Nobody likes ego-driven leaders. Worse, they resent them. We all have flaws; it's a matter of humility if we are willing, in a manner of speaking, to stop being ourselves and quit acting out those flaws. As Friedrich Nietzsche once said, "Sometimes people don't want to hear the truth because they don't want their illusions destroyed." I'm not advocating for people to pretend to be something they are not. I'm asking them to recognize their ego-driven flaws and stop leading that way.

> As a leader, I see myself as a playful sheepdog—
> but ready to take on the wolf.

From Suggestion Box to Leading Outside the Box

If you are afraid to open that suggestion box and read its contents, you're probably not doing something right. Complaints that come out of the box tend to be universal. And if you're not convinced a suggestion box will get you all the information you need, you're probably right. Spending more time with your teams, appraising verbal and nonverbal behavior, and simply asking questions will also help.

> Go see your subordinates.
> Don't always expect them to come see you.

When I compared my lessons learned with my friend Gail Brooks, who has spent more than 30 years consulting on and teaching leadership, we found similar flaws in what I call "ego-based leadership" in both the SEAL Teams and in the business world. In this case, stopping certain things is as important as "doing something about it."

The common flaws of ego-based leadership include these:

1. Taking credit for other people's work

2. Not listening

3. Criticizing the negative; ignoring the positive

4. Asking for input after you've already made the decision

5. Micromanaging

6. Not having your subordinates' backs

7. Not following your own policies

8. Not having the courage to give bad news to your boss

9. Trying to always be right

10. Wearing your emotions on your sleeve, particularly anger

11. Being a martyr and complaining about everything

12. Not respecting your subordinates' time

13. Keeping people in the dark

14. Not prioritizing (everything is important)

15. Wasting other people's time

16. Never accepting blame

17. Making promises and not following through

18. Not recognizing small gains; only focusing on the big win and bottom line

19. Not recognizing that people have lives outside of work

20. Playing favorites

21. Not apologizing or admitting wrongdoing

This list is hardly all-inclusive. As you read the list, I'm sure you could empathize and see some of those traits in yourself, your boss, or your boss's boss. I think back on some of the leaders who I've served under. The farther back I go, the less I remember what I did and the more I remember how the leaders treated me and how they led. What does *that* say?

The ones that were self-serving—there weren't many—I thank God are in my past. But the ones that led as humble servant leaders, I look back on with reverence, and I treasure the fond memories. Remember, humility requires us to divorce our egos, but it doesn't mean that we don't care about our egos. We stay in touch with them; we just don't let them run our lives.

> **Mutual respect and dignity spark the spirit of leadership and compassion.**

Being a Leader Should Never Hurt

I've started more than one chapter with stories or anecdotes calling into question the necessity and priority of killing, and whether or not it is easy to do. It isn't. Not even for SEALs, it isn't. It isn't what we're about; killing is done only to preserve ourselves and/or to accomplish our mission. The idea extends beyond "kill" to "hurt." It accomplishes nothing to hurt someone, particularly someone on your team or in your unit. It creates bad feelings between you and that person and introduces fear. And we've seen where that fear leads: to ego. And then what? More examples of power, more fear—you see where this is going.

If you stop and think about how any action (or inaction) on your part can, or will, hurt someone, inside or outside your team, you'll go much further as a leader.

Stop, look, and empathize.

TAKEAWAYS

- Leaders need to be humble, to consider others first.

- "Humility is not thinking less of yourself. It's about thinking of yourself less."

- Leadership is something you do *with* people, not *to* them.

- Fear, if not channeled, breeds ego, which brings negative consequences to leadership.

- The opposite of fear is love. Practice leadership more of love and less of ego.

- In servant leadership, if you take care of the needs of others, they will take care of your needs and those of the team.

- Servant leadership is about the team first.

- When people operate in fear of you, they shut down, or worse, spend energy creating false impressions.

- Open communication, skits, suggestion boxes, and just being with your teams are all good ways of appraising your own behaviors as a leader.

- Fear, ego, and pain tend to bring more fear, ego, and pain. As a leader, you must avoid this cycle.

CHAPTER 6

Always On:
Leadership in the
Moment, Every Moment

Just prior to 9/11, when I was the Third Phase Training
Officer at BUD/S, I worked for one of the best leaders
I've ever known. He possessed all the traits that I spoke of in
the last chapter: humble, human, genuine. He commanded
what we call "the school house." It's our center for basic and
advanced training. This is a major command (only a Navy
Captain, one step below Admiral, can be in command). To
protect his privacy, I'll refer to him as Mr. Rick—normally
I would call him "Sir," not out of duty but out of respect for
him as a great officer and leader.

As members of a relatively small community, everyone
in the SEAL Teams knows or has heard of everyone else.
Your reputation is very valuable, but it can be detrimental as
well. In the SEAL Teams, you can tell who the great leaders
are by how many people request orders into their command.
Generally, officers change jobs and commands every two
years. When officers come up for a new assignment, they
get what we call a "dream sheet" on which to list their three

top choices for jobs. The process for detailing officers is political, and like most things we deal with, it has plenty of VUCA. The career of each officer must be managed to hit the mandated milestone jobs for promotion. Some jobs are considered "hard fill" and some are considered "good deals." After you finish a hard fill, you get "a good deal for a good SEAL," as we say. You know what you'll get after a good deal.

Surprisingly, being in the training command is considered a hard fill; it's very difficult to get SEALs to volunteer for it. The reason is simple: SEALs want to be doing SEAL stuff, not training a bunch of "tadpoles who want to be frogmen." Combat positions for officers are considered good deals. In the military we give orders for, not invitations to, assignments.

When we found out that Mr. Rick was selected to run the training command, the requests for orders into the command poured in. Like most SEALs, Mr. Rick didn't want to come to the training command. He wanted to command one of our classified combat units. He had spent around 15 years, what we call "being on the beeper," standing by to deploy at any time in one of our most secretive commands. He had paid his dues, but instead of getting the job that he wanted, he got the training command.

Nonetheless, Mr. Rick's reputation beat him to the command by a month or so. Everyone was excited and willing to do a hard fill job in order to work for a great leader. General Stanley McChrystal, who famously resigned the Afghanistan command under President Obama, had the same reputation. Both of these great leaders had extremely high expectations of their people; they weren't loved for having a vacation at work! People would take the tough jobs just to serve under them. Of course the opposite is true as well. Some take the tough jobs just to avoid a self-serving leader.

I learned a lot about myself and about leadership during my first performance review (what we call "counseling") with Mr. Rick. Normally the counseling sessions are short and mostly one-way; the leader explains the evaluation he gave you. At that point, I had been in the military for nine years and was used to counseling, so I didn't expect such a thorough talk with the Captain. He explained in detail what he saw in me and what he knew my reputation to be. It's rare for someone to give you an honest assessment of your overall reputation. It's also very valuable to know something about yourself, something that others know and you don't.

I didn't know it, but before this counseling, he had done his homework. He had made calls and had studied my record. In some ways, I felt as if he had been spying on me! He gave me the good news first and talked about my reputation as a leader and as what we call a "good operator." Then we turned to the other side of my reputation. Let's call that my "upward reputation," also known in business parlance as "opportunities." That's where it got really interesting.

So what am I getting at? Simply this: leadership is not one thing you do. It's *everything* you do. Leaders should understand that they are on stage all the time and that their people are watching and judging every aspect of their actions, in and out of the office. As a leader, you must not leave your reputation or their perception of you up to chance. Take the offensive mindset and strike first. This is an important part of the First, Fast, Fearless leadership Brand.

> **Leadership is not one thing you do.**
> **It's *everything* you do.**

Perception Management: Leadership Happens in the Minds of Others

In that first counseling session, Mr. Rick and I discussed what he referred to as "perception management." It not only applies to your followers but also to your leaders. He informed me that if I wanted to be aggressive with my own reputation, I would need to be seen by senior officers on the "battlefield" that I had created. When he probed within the community, my name was not well known among the senior officers. He let me know that just as on the battlefield, leaders needed to put themselves in the best position to make the best decisions; in this case, it meant to be seen by senior officers.

In short, you must market yourself. I'll be the first to say that this is not in my true nature; furthermore, I am not advocating that leaders need to be schmoozers, social butterflies, or ass-kissers. I'm saying that it's important to treat your reputation with an offensive, first strike mentality. Be the cause of it, not the effect, and by all means, don't let chance dictate it. Just as with Mr. Rick, if you build a solid reputation, people will come running because great leaders develop fans and a following.

> **You build it and they will come. Leaders don't just lead. They build a following.**

"Oh Shit!" Management

While playing offense in the reputation game, it's important to play a little defense too. Not only should you consistently move forward with a first strike mindset in what you do *and* with others' *perceptions* of what you do, but you must also avoid big mistakes. Word about those mistakes will get around. And if you do make a mistake, how you manage it is critical.

In the vernacular of business, *damage control* is important. But just what is damage control? It is (1) admitting the mistake and (2) finding a way forward, quickly, to correct it. So many get stuck in the blame game, or "find the fault," or finding out *who* was at fault. In our environment and in any organizational environment that has an appetite for risk, it's easier to admit your mistakes and move on than to expend energy covering them up or finding someone else to own them.

As Warren Buffett famously said, "It takes years to build a reputation and only minutes to ruin it."

Getting to Know Them

Leaders need to know their people personally and professionally. I learned early in my career to constantly log or write down what people do, good and bad, so that the counseling is meaningful and accurate. I used to keep a log of people's family and personal lives, as well as details of their performance. Great leaders let their people know what goes into the log along the way to avoid surprises at counseling time. If I gave someone a bad review, it came as no surprise because he already knew it was coming, so he had no problems accepting it, and he took more positive corrective actions more quickly.

Being a Leader—and Looking the Part

Every time an officer goes up for a selected position board, a full-length picture of him in uniform goes up onto the big screen for all to see. The room is full of his senior officers; they all have a covered keypad with which to score each officer discretely. These meetings are secret in nature and are unannounced. No one knows who is participating.

A photo is taken of every SEAL in the same uniform, with the same backdrop, and by the same type of camera—all conditions are the same. We want to think that the way we look doesn't matter, but we all know it does. For SEALs, a clear sign of self-control or self-leadership is staying fit. Our job requires us to use our bodies to complete the mission, so taking care of ourselves is part of the job. We have a saying: "Take care of your gear and your gear (in this case, your body) will take care of you." We are all on a stage in life, like it or not.

I learned a lot about perception management from a fellow SEAL I'll call Ray. For the most part, as an officer, Ray was in the middle of the pack. To get selected to try out to be a SEAL Officer is extremely competitive, and those who are selected excelled at top universities and were often competitive athletes as well. So I'm not insulting Ray by saying he was in the middle of an elite pack. His intelligence, leadership, and tactical proficiency were good, but compared to his peers, he was unexceptional.

What Ray had was the "package," so to speak. He was tall, lean, and muscular, and he always looked the part. He was a great speaker and was always well prepared when meeting with senior officers. Physically, he was gifted. He could run and swim fast, and he was as strong as an ox for his size. He looked like a SEAL. He always found a way to get senior officers to do physical training with him or to be in their presence to make the desired impression.

Over the years, I heard senior officers talk about him and how great he was as a SEAL leader. Ray consistently placed in the top 10 percent against his peers. The perception of him by the senior officers who ranked him was significantly higher than his actual abilities as a SEAL leader. He was promoted to the top and is now one of the most senior officers in the SEAL community.

As leaders, we have our own Brand. It's a personal Brand, and in our case, it's the SEAL Brand. It's a Brand we should hold dear to our hearts. Be very proactive, with an offensive mindset, about maintaining that Brand.

> **Personal discipline is a great leadership tool. If you're sloppy and unprepared, people will notice and judge you accordingly.**

The Sound of a Leader: Leadership on Stage

You can be wrong as a leader, but that said, you should stay away from speaking of doubt. Over the years, I've picked up the ability to spot a Navy SEAL, an Admiral, or a General out of uniform in a crowd. Senior leaders develop a style and language that staff people don't have. It's noticeable in a room even when everyone is out of uniform.

Leaders need to watch their language, but they also need to have an offensive mindset when speaking. "Trying," "thinking," or "guessing" are just verbal ways of not taking responsibility for the results. You may have doubts and complaints, but you do no one any favors by expressing them to your subordinates. People need leaders to express competence and confidence, to be forward thinking, clear, concise, and definite.

Public speaking is part of our professional leadership development program. All officers and enlisted SEALs study and learn public speaking. It's a skill that every leader must have. The higher you go, the greater must be your mastery of this skill because you have more influence and less contact with the employees. When you do have contact with your people, it's important that you can speak and express yourself clearly. Your competence will also be judged by how well you can engage and speak to your team. Think about how they would want to receive the message.

Most people report that public speaking is one of their biggest fears and avoid it when possible. If you train to do it, you can inoculate yourself against that fear. Better yet, turn fear into opportunity.

There's no doubt that what works in the SEAL world also works in the enterprise. Speak forward, speak clearly, speak concisely, and be definite.

Putting It in Writing

People communicate more and more by email than in person or on the phone. Being deliberate with your writing and what you put out into the world is also critical. We've all received emails that made us wonder how the sender ever graduated from elementary school; or the emails that unintentionally pissed us off for days. Emails can be easily misunderstood, and they are often confusing, so be clear, and don't be afraid to follow up important ones with a phone call.

You can tell a lot about a person from an email. You can spot the person who is multitasking and can't focus, the one who is delaying a decision and just voicing his opinion, the one who copies everyone with attachments to pass on responsibility and culpability. Perception of you and your competence will be viewed through the quality and quantity of everything you write. Be intentional with emails or with any other written correspondence because they are permanent.

Again, be forward, clear, concise, and definite. Perception matters. Even your email persona is on stage for review.

Don't Dress More Warmly Than Your People

General George Patton was famous for his leadership style. He believed that general officers must be careful not to appear to be dressed more warmly than the troops. People loved and hated him at the same time, but General Patton knew, among other things, that perception mattered, especially the higher up you go. Of course, he meant that leaders should share the burden and not take special privileges.

The higher you go, the less contact you have with the organization. When you are highly ranked, every contact, even for a moment, means something and adds to the perception of your leadership. A CEO shouldn't show up at the factory with a gold Rolex. They all know you make more money than they do, but leave the watch at home. Don't show off your power and prestige, especially to those who likely had a lot to do with it but don't enjoy the same benefits. Be one with your team.

That said, it's also disingenuous to pretend you *are* them. It may be perceived as not genuine or even condescending. They know you are not one of them. Yet they can and will respect you if they feel their well-being is your concern and you have their backs:

On one of my tours in Iraq, I noticed that when traveling from city to city, the Marine Generals drove in the convoys with the grunts. Most of the other Generals of the Army and Air Force, as well as the Admirals of the Navy, flew from city to city instead of driving in the streets.

I understand that for Admirals and Generals, time is valuable, and flying in a helicopter from Baghdad to Fallujah is much faster than driving. But the grunts have to drive because air assets are few and far between, and they have to move equipment. Marine Generals understood what Patton was talking about. At the height of the war, everyone knew that driving in a convoy posed a significant risk of hitting an improvised explosive device (IED) and getting blown up.

These Marine Generals understood that soldier perceptions mattered to the effectiveness of their leadership, so they told their Marines that they too would suffer the burden and risks of combat. I've heard Marines talk about how that act alone helped to build the legend of a great leader. I have the utmost respect for Marine leadership up and down the chain of command.

As a SEAL Officer, you are not considered a "laborer"—and enlisted men let you know that. Although we go through BUD/S training side by side with the enlisted and endure the same hardships, when we get to the teams, we specialize in leading and planning. But every officer understands that if the troops are out building and packing equipment for a training trip or deployment and we aren't planning or engaged in some other leadership activity, we go outside and get dirty with the troops. And we don't go out there as a leader or foreman. We do what the senior enlisted SEAL in charge of the process tells us to do. We get dirty, which is a great way to show respect. They know we have a different job, but we all share the load.

Power by example, not examples of power.

> Leadership occurs in concentric rings.
> What you do as a leader resonates throughout
> the organization.

Leadership Moments: When the Bugle Sounds

Leadership is not one thing you do. It's everything you do. But some moments are more important than others. They make a strategic impact on your leadership effect on the team and your reputation. These are the *leadership moments* that happen throughout the course of your career, and they are shining opportunities to make the most of your leadership responsibility.

In training, we say, "Everybody wants to be a frogman on a sunny day." When people aren't wet, cold, and miserable, they want to be a SEAL. That also applies to being a leader. Leadership is a choice that you make, not something that someone else gives you, such as rank, position, or any other privilege.

The expression "when the bugle sounds" refers to the call to war in the days of the cavalry. I use that term to signify a moment when leadership truly matters. Your reputation will be defined by these precious moments. For your people, these moments are those of conflict, stress, fear, and VUCA. Will you stand up and face that challenge?

> Be in the moment during times of stress.

If this sounds like an impossible feat, it's not. It merely means that you must recognize these moments in time, understand your emotions, control them and your actions, and stand up. Great leaders understand the importance of not losing their composure during difficult times. They understand that it is at these times when their people rely on them the most. Nobody needs a leader when it's easy, but they will want and need one when it's hard. People are hypersensitive to leadership when the stress dial is turned up.

> **Everyone who wants to be a leader should be there in times of adversity.**

I was fortunate to have learned this lesson early on, when I was going through BUD/S training. During Hellweek, the instructors constantly reminded us that if it were easy, everyone would do it. After days of no sleep and constantly being wet and sandy, they reinforced that the time for leaders to excel is during these terrible moments when everyone is under immense pressure, both physically and psychologically.

This lesson was critical during one of my deployments to Iraq. I was starting a new Task Unit in Ramadi. The mission had changed, and, honestly, we didn't have a clearly stated mission at all. The requirements for launching also weren't clearly defined. It was the ultimate state of VUCA, and our resources and assets were sorely limited. Doesn't this sound like modern business life?

It was like trying to build an airplane in flight. We had to clearly define our priorities and efforts. Of course, none of this is as hard as figuring out the personal issues that come up and diffusing the problems as they arise. The concept of the leadership moment was front of mind constantly. I refused to allow myself to fall apart during the greatest moments of stress. I knew that the team needed someone to be strong, someone to be a voice of reason and reassurance.

> **In stressful conditions, people are hypersensitive to leadership.**

97

A few months later, after we finally got our Battle Rhythm, one of my senior enlisted SEALs came into my office and thanked me for being calm and making sense out of the chaos. He complimented me on my ability to be calm in the face of so much VUCA. It was a great moment and a pat on the back I needed at the time. Little did he know that I was like a duck on a pond, calm on the surface but paddling like hell underneath!

Getting it right during these leadership moments is not about being the most courageous, the toughest, or even the most qualified. It's about choosing to accept the privilege and responsibility of leadership and to stand up to address problems head on, with a first strike mindset—with a First, Fast, Fearless mentality.

TAKEAWAYS

- Leadership is not one thing you do. It is *everything* you do.

- Perception is reality; managing others' perceptions of you is very important.

- Treat your reputation with an offensive, first strike mentality. Leave nothing to chance.

- When you make a mistake, admit it and take the offensive to correct it.

- As a leader, you're always on stage. How you look, sound, and write matters.

- Always speak forward, speak clearly, speak concisely, and be definite. The same goes for what you write.

- Don't overpower your people with privilege, and don't go overboard trying to be "one of them." Stick with putting their needs first.

- Leaders are most needed in times of adversity, and they are most respected for what they do then.

CHAPTER 7

Look, Listen, and Feel: Communication and Charisma Fight Side by Side

I was designated the reconnaissance team leader in one platoon. Reconnaissance work is done in small teams and often in highly hostile enemy environments and long distances from friendly force, as we saw in the film *Lone Survivor*.

Most of the time, reconnaissance missions involve snipers who have had rigorous training and have mastered what we call "field craft." Field craft is the operator's ability to effectively live in the field undetected for long periods of time. For the most part, such missions are tedious and take great concentration and discipline. They are often boring, yet they can get very dangerous very quickly.

The more you know about tactics and the environment you're in, the better chance you have for mission success. We SEALs understand we don't know everything about warfare or tactics, but we are learners willing to learn anything to become a better operator to succeed at the mission.

So I sought out the best training possible to supplement my current training program. I found a man who had been trained in tracking by an elder Apache scout. I learned that the scout had trained other SEALs in tracking and field craft during the period of the Vietnam War. He had spent years living in the woods, tracking not only animals but also criminals and lost hikers.

One of the snipers on the team traveled with me to meet the Native American tracker in the Pine Barrens of New Jersey and spend time living and training in the woods. Although I knew the scout had a great reputation as one of the best trackers in the world, I was skeptical of the claims he made about his ability to track any animal on any surface. But I was prepared for anything.

We started by learning the different names given to different parts of any track left on the ground or any surface that had been disturbed. He claimed that there were several thousand signs that gave details about individual animals from the tracks they left, anything from their type and sex to their condition. It all seemed a little hokey to us, but we immersed ourselves in what he was saying and learned all we could.

He practiced many of the traditions of Native Americans, such as the use of sweat lodges, "fox walking," stalking, building tools from nature, and living off the land. One of the first tracking experiments we did took place inside the old barn located on the property. The barn was full of antlers, buck skins, and tracking boxes made of packed sand to practice seeing specific markings that animals leave; the barn was our classroom.

In front of the classroom stood an ordinary wooden table with a flat surface that would be used for our first tracking lesson. He had one of his helpers walk across the table in shoes to see if we could find the tracks. Of course I couldn't see anything, and it looked just as I thought it would—undisturbed. We looked it over for a period of time; there was no sign of a track. Nothing. The tracker walked over to the barn door, turned off the light, and opened the side barn door. The sun was getting low in the sky.

With the sun hitting the table at an angle, we could clearly see the footprints on the table. The light had cast a slight shadow on the disturbed dirt. The tracks stuck out plain as day! The fact is, dust settles on the earth, and if it's disturbed, signs are left behind. We started to become believers.

Under his guidance, we started to do some tracking exercises of our own. The first exercise was to try and find field mouse tracks. He would locate the tracks for us so that we knew where to start looking. For hours we had our faces in the dirt. It wasn't until we spent those hours in the dirt that we finally began to see the tracks. When we did, they looked like elephant tracks.

Eventually he put us on larger animal tracks—squirrels, rabbits, and foxes. These tracks didn't take as much work to find and follow, even on surfaces like grass and pine needles. As we progressed and logged in more hours with our faces in the dirt, it became easier to locate the tracks of small animals with little effort. Before we knew it, we could see the tracks from a standing position. We could now see the disturbance in the earth, ever so slight, but we knew it had been disturbed.

Picking Up the Subliminal

The tracks reminded me of the subliminal messages I was obsessed with as a child. I would stare at liquor ads in magazines until I could see the hidden words and objects in them. Still today when I go into a convenience store and see the cigarettes behind the counter, I see the image of a man in "all his glory" facing backward on the pack of Camel cigarettes. The tracks popped out at me just like the subliminal messages in advertisements. Once you see it, you always see it.

Leadership is subtle. Like the animal tracks described above, you won't see it—until you *do*. Once you see leadership, you always see it. The tracks are both overt and subliminal. Once you're a leader and consistently exhibit leadership traits, you're always a leader. Your people will undergo the same transformation: once they see you as a leader, they will always see you as a leader.

Part of the challenge is, of course, to leave the right tracks.

> **Once you see leadership, you always see it.**

A New Awareness: Look, Listen, and Feel

The same time we were learning to track, we also studied nature and lived in the woods. We paid attention to the sounds of nature and how animals react when other animals come into the area. The concentric rings of nature are there; you just have to observe them and understand the connection. If a fox is sneaking in the area, the squirrels will take to the trees, and the birds will fly off; it's all connected.

By the time we were finished at Pine Barrens, we had gained far more than just tracking skills. We had gained a new awareness of nature and the interconnection of it all. This new awareness was invaluable to leadership and, specifically, to how I communicated with my team. Communication is the thread that holds us all together in life and at work. The expression "look, listen, and feel" comes from the idea that when you make an insertion into enemy territory, you need all of your senses to be working in a heightened state. You need to pay attention to everything.

> **Good leaders evaluate what's going on with all six senses before they step in. Their sixth sense is their personal experience.**

From the moment the helicopter or boat inserts your team into the field, you take cover and concealment, forming a 360-degree perimeter. You completely stop moving and stay silent. You look for any signs of enemies; you listen not only to the sounds of people but also to the sounds of nature. When nature is disturbed, it leaves signs. At the moment of insertion, the wildlife and insects become quiet because the noise scares them. We sit there motionless until the chorus of nature restarts, so we know we are not in an ambush. We use all of our senses to feel what is going on around us.

HOOYAH!

Aside from direct communication from speaker to listener, subtle, subliminal, and reflex communications back to the speaker are important. Communication is a two-way street, and it can be subtle, abbreviated, and/or nonverbal in both directions.

We have an expression that we use as a battle cry; in BUD/S training, it's an acknowledgment of directions given. For instance, if you ask, "Do you understand what I'm saying to you?" students answer with a short, sharp "HOOYAH!" meaning yes, they do. Students get very creative with this battle cry and use it in different ways just by changing the tone of their voice. We might ask, "Are you an idiot?" and the response would be HOOYAH! (meaning of course not, you are the idiot!).

To effectively communicate and understand what people say and what they mean, we must pay attention and focus on their *intent*; that is, we must be aware. It's like finding that track in the dust. It's not just the words that are said. It's how they're said and what they really mean. Be aware, know what's going on, know what's going on behind what's going on. Always try to peek behind the curtain.

Body Language and Listening

If you have ever watched a poker championship, you know the importance of body language and how it can give away what you are really thinking. Most of the great poker players wear dark sunglasses and develop a card-handling routine because they don't want their opponents to see the subtle telltale signs of their hand.

I believe that most people in the working world aren't very attuned to their body language. Most do little or nothing to control it; they just don't pay much attention to it in the preparation or delivery of their message.

When you do pay attention, you can watch for simple universal signs of anger, joy, surprise, sadness, disgust, contempt, and fear. The University of California at San Diego did a study of SEALs and "normal" people and found that SEALs were considerably more able to recognize anger in people.

> Great leaders are great listeners and can hear—
> or sense—people's fears. Anger, resentment,
> and frustration are all symptoms of fear.

In meetings, I used to make a point to control my movements, so as not to give away too much nonverbal information, some of which might have been harmful. I also made an effort not to stare at my notes. If you watch the room, you can learn a lot more than you think.

Deploying a Listening Buddy

Every SEAL officer has a "better-half" subordinate in his unit, a Senior Enlisted Advisor (SEA) who goes where he goes and sits in meetings with him. During these meetings, the SEA pays attention to the room and looks around to see how the message is being received. He looks for "tracks" I might have missed. After each meeting, my SEA and I would always debrief and talk about how it went and what he saw. His job is to watch people and not only to hear what they say but also to figure out how they felt and what they meant. His job is to feel the pulse of the meeting and the team.

What You're About to Hear Is Free

It's important not only to listen closely and make sure you're getting the message—both the spoken message and the tracks around it—but also to make the time and effort to listen in the first place. So many of us forget that. What you're about to hear is free—you just have to tune in!

Repeat After You

When listening to people, I often repeat back to them what I heard—or really, what I think they meant. It's a way of truly opening up the conversation and getting away from just the words. When people see that you are paying attention to them, it improves the interaction because they know you are listening. Always look to find their intent and then strike first to (1) make sure you know what they meant and (2) let your intent be known.

> When listening to someone, don't get distracted by phones, computers, or visitors. Shut the door or find a quiet place. Otherwise, you'll waste your time and theirs.

Give Honest Feedback, and Don't Find the Fault

One of the most important—and most sensitive—tasks that leaders have, whether in the SEAL world or in the business world, is to give feedback to our troops and our teams. The leader who can't make the time or effort to do this, well, isn't a leader.

Feedback, of course, gets everyone better aligned on whatever is being discussed—the values, the mission, or specific tasks undertaken by the team. People want to know how they're doing; they seek security in what they do and how they approach their responsibility.

Without that feedback or with feedback that is delivered in the wrong way, people struggle with self-doubt about their performance or their role in the team. Feedback is important, it should be given, and it should be given in the *right way*. Giving it in the right way means being clear and being honest, telling people what they did right as well as what they did wrong.

I'm sure you've seen them—power-tripping leaders quick to bite off someone's head when he or she makes the slightest mistake, leaders who use the feedback process to build and assert their power. These power plays can happen even with leaders who seem well balanced otherwise. It seems that at feedback time they always find the fault, out of insecurity or a need to demonstrate they're on top or better qualified than their subordinates to do the task. Highly insecure leaders think their job is to "find the fault," and they spend most of their time doing that. In my book, these individuals aren't leaders. When they find fault with their subordinates publicly, that is, in front of everyone else, look out below.

> **Never disrespect people personally or publicly.**
> **If you do, apologize quickly.**

Remember, be honest, balance the positive and the negative, be clear, and take your own ego out of it. The people receiving the feedback will get more out of the process in the short term, and everyone will benefit in the long term.

> When complimenting someone or approving
> something, don't use the words *but* or *however*.
> You're probably looking for perfection in things
> that don't matter.

Emotional Intelligence, Not Ego

As the Training Officer for all West Coast Navy SEAL Teams, one of my jobs was to develop what we call "readiness." *Readiness* is a blanket term covering everything it takes to get SEALs ready to deploy. It includes practices such as yoga, meditation, biofeedback, supplementation, and marriage counseling, among others. We held family retreats at Disneyland with experts from the above specialties to try and help SEALs, support staff, and families deal with the pressure of sustained combat. What we sought were aids to increase readiness and resilience. Resilience training was part of what we call the "whole man" approach to leadership. We know that the whole person comes to work and goes to war.

As I was doing research for the resilience program, I realized how much resilience depended on leadership and certain leadership qualities. I read the *Harvard Business Review* article "What Makes a Leader?" by Daniel Goleman, the author of *Emotional Intelligence: Why It Can Matter More Than IQ.*

In his study of nearly 200 large global companies, Goleman found that while the qualities traditionally associated with leadership—intelligence, toughness, determination, and vision—are required for success, they are insufficient. Truly effective leaders are also distinguished by a high degree of emotional intelligence, which includes self-awareness, self-regulation, motivation, empathy, and social skill.

There's a very important distinction between "successful" and "effective." I've seen successful leaders scorch and burn their people. After two years, they left, and the staff was ineffective, with low engagement and varied performance. They may have been "successful" at getting the job done, but were they "effective"?

Effective leaders push their people hard, but they bounce back better for it. Leaders who allow themselves to lead with their egos may be successful in the short term but ineffective in the longer term. Money can buy only so much motivation. Beyond that, insecure, egotistical, and emotionally numb leaders build fear. That fear overtakes the motivation produced by the compensation. Fear consumes the team; everyone avoids everyone else, especially the boss.

It may sound strange to you that a SEAL is talking about the importance of emotional intelligence. But keep in mind, we are *all* human and made of the same stuff. We share 99.9 percent of our DNA! Understanding the value of empathy and being able to feel what people are saying (and what tracks they're leaving) has been a valuable tool for me. It begins with being aware, patient, and not quick to judge—truly empathetic. It really works.

Charisma

We've discussed how to have a more effective two-way relationship with employees or team members. Do they look forward to hearing what you have to say or observing how you do something? Would they rather have you around than *not* have you around? Do they not only respect you but also *like* you? Would they come to your funeral (other than to get the day off)? Now we approach the Holy Grail of "side by side" First, Fast, Fearless leadership: *charisma*.

I've heard people talk about how President Clinton had charisma and how he seemed to always remember or comment on something personal about people whenever he saw them. His ability to look, listen, and feel in all situations gave him a certain flair that is hard to mimic. President Clinton has always been a very good listener; he makes people feel the conversation is in their court, so to speak. He's not scary; he doesn't let his ego get in the way, and he doesn't talk down to people. He makes time and pays the respect due to anyone he talks to.

Again, power by example, not examples of power.

Listening is not about waiting for your turn to talk when you are a leader. It's about getting results. Effective leaders realize that they already know what they know. They want to hear from their people to learn what they *don't* know—it's a priority.

Over the years, I've made a lot of mistakes and have allowed my ego to creep in when it should have been left at the door. If you drop your ego and pay attention to small signs of communication, you'll see the tracks and grasp true intent:

> When I was the Third Phase Officer at BUD/S training in charge of teaching weapons, explosives, and tactics, one of my senior instructors was a man I'll call Chief Mike. Chief Mike was a decorated and wounded Vietnam veteran. This was prior to 9/11. All of us younger SEALs were in awe of these guys, and rightfully so. Although there were operations going on around the world, they were not the sustained combat situations of Vietnam—or Iraq and Afghanistan years later.
>
> Chief Mike had left the SEALs around 20 years prior, and he was a schoolteacher before he came back in. Like most SEALs, he missed the Brotherhood of the SEAL Teams, so he decided to rejoin the organization. Twenty years away is a long time for any constantly evolving profession, especially one like the SEAL Teams. One of his jokes with the younger SEALs was, "I've forgotten more than you know." We know that the technical skills learned as a SEAL are perishable.
>
> Chief Mike was in charge of tactics, which is one of the most involved portions of training. As the SEAL, you are in charge of the other SEALs in your department, and you are

supposed to not only lead them but also be the subject matter expert.

Quickly, I began to see that Chief Mike was behind. When we spoke to him about it, he was secretive and guarded about his job. I started to realize that he didn't possess enough confidence in doing his job. In his position, there is no time to learn it. It's expected that you know your job and can hit the ground running. My SEA approached me; we both knew that we needed to confront him.

My SEA called Chief Mike in for a counseling, and before I could even express myself, he was visibly angry and full of contempt. One of his first comments was, "God damn, I can't believe I'm getting counseled by someone younger than my daughter." Well, that surprised me, and for a moment I was at a loss for words. I decided that I had not done my due diligence and had not prepared for this conversation. I ended the session and went back to my room to prepare myself.

This was a man older than my dad. He was a wounded decorated hero, and I was about to fire him. Moral courage is important. I knew I had to do the right thing. But at the same time, I had put him in a position to fail, and I was accountable for that. I spent hours preparing my next meeting but remembered how embarrassed he was. Shame is one of the strongest emotions; it's like an extra strong drug or a high-powered special weapon. For strong teams, shame is one of the worst things that can happen.

As a leader, you have to earn the right to fire someone, and that person has to deserve it as well. Leaders must give people the right tools to succeed; people respond by living up to standards. But this situation with Chief Mike was different; he didn't have time to get caught up on his job. We had placed him in a job he wasn't equipped for, and we had left him unprepared.

I understood what he was saying by his actions and his

tone, and I could empathize with his feelings of shame. At our next counseling, I asked him to let me speak for a few minutes. I explained in detail what I had seen and heard, and I explained how I thought he felt. I let him know that I had put him in a bad position and that I knew his competence and confidence were low and that he was scared of being shamed. I reached out to him from a position of respect and understanding.

After 15 minutes or so, I saw his body respond with relief. The first thing he said to me was, "Thank you, sir. You are absolutely right." My SEA and I were both a little disarmed; we didn't expect this reaction. But he knew that I respected and cared about him and that I took responsibility for putting him in a bad position. This was the first time someone thanked me for firing him!

He was a hero, a great leader and a great team player, and he had years of experience. So I asked him to run the camp and mentor the students, especially the young officers. He thrived; the students loved him and couldn't wait for him to speak to them.

This reinforced for me that leadership is personal and that understanding how others feel is as important as understanding how I feel. I know you cannot always find another position for someone you have to fire, but doing your due diligence as a leader and respecting people sends a message throughout the organization.

In that leadership moment, I feel like I had hit a home run. I was able to diffuse a potentially hostile engagement and turn it into a win-win by putting my ego aside, empathizing with another person, and using all of my senses. I studied the tracks and spoke to him through his eyes, not my own.

> **Charisma is the opposite of ego.**

Several years later, I was on the bay side of the Silver Strand in Coronado, California, when Chief Mike crossed the street and flagged me down. He once again thanked me for what I had done years earlier and invited me to his house for his retirement party. But I soon deployed to Afghanistan and couldn't make it.

Leadership moments matter. Pay attention and look for the tracks, be close to your people, show emotional intelligence, and manage your charisma and character—and that of others—for the best. It's all part of the First, Fast, Fearless leadership Brand.

TAKEAWAYS

- Be aware, think awareness, and try creative new ways to expand your awareness.

- If you tune in to subtle and subliminal messages, you'll communicate far more effectively. Always look for the "tracks."

- Once you see leadership, you always see it.

- Always add the "sixth sense," experience, to the other five.

- Great leaders are great listeners.

- Tap the power of others to expand your listening "ears."

- Listen actively; put your ego in check.

- Give balanced, regular, clear, concise, and honest feedback. Don't shame anyone publicly, and again, put your ego in check.

- Emotional intelligence—self-awareness, self-regulation, motivation, empathy, and social skills—will make you a more effective leader.

CHAPTER 8

"Ya Got What Ya Got": Leading Through Bureaucracy and Limited Resources

By the time 9/11 happened, the military as a whole had been virtually stagnant for decades and hadn't been involved in a sustained war since Vietnam. In Iraq and Afghanistan, we found that the enemy had no battle lines, was elusive, and was embedded within the civilian population.

As SEAL warriors, we knew that we had courage, teamability, and the ability to solve problems. Fighting two completely separate wars tested our forces to their limits. There was no playbook, and after Saddam Hussein was toppled, the military looked around and said, "Now what?"

It's apparent now that we didn't have a clear and concise campaign plan for Iraq after the 2003 invasion. The insurgency became a long and deadly fight. The conventional military did a world-class job of storming through Iraq, faster than any military in the history of warfare, but there was much more to be done.

Special Operations Forces (SOF) live by five truths:

1. Humans are more important than hardware.

2. Quality is better than quantity.

3. Special Operations Forces cannot be mass produced.

4. Special Operations require non-SOF assistance.

5. Competent Special Operations Forces cannot be created after emergencies occur.

When 9/11 happened, everyone in the Special Operations world understood that "ya got what ya got." For years, we would live with the forces we had because you cannot grow overnight. It takes two and a half years to train a SEAL before his first deployment and more years to mature him for the many special activities we conduct.

Naturally, right after the attacks, the budget for the Special Operations Command (SOCOM) skyrocketed for all Special Operations Forces. But bureaucracy within the Department of Defense is strong, so at times, it's almost impossible to spend the money that you get—even for Special Operations!

For over a decade to come, all forces would be undermanned, overworked, and required to do more with less; it became a way of life. Not only were we fighting two insurgencies in Iraq and Afghanistan but we also had an operation in the Philippines and we were in pursuit of terrorists around the world. Everything was changing constantly. And yet, we were locked into what we had. Part of the SEAL leadership Brand is to deal with those constraints and to move forward as best you can. Leadership is getting people to want to—and be able to—do something important. The task at hand was to keep them wanting to and still able to—you can't sit around waiting to get dealt a better hand.

> **Never focus on getting dealt a better hand.**

It Starts with Accountability

I hear the term *accountability* thrown around in every seminar I'm in. But most who use it haven't made it clear to their people what accountability really means, nor have they set the conditions for people to be accountable. Dealing with limited resources—and getting things done anyway—requires accountability.

In the military and any productive organization, accountability as a leader is critical and is enforced at all levels. When you accept command, when you are in charge, everything rests on you. As SEAL leaders, we know and accept this when we join.

> **Dealing with limited resources—**
> **and getting things done anyway—**
> **is a sign of accountability.**

Some people confuse the terms *responsibility* and *accountability*. You can be responsible and also accountable, but the two are not one and the same. Responsibility is what I call "pointing the finger," that is, finding the cause when something goes wrong; it's what most organizations do. It's identifying who made the mistake and blaming that person or people. Accountability is not about who is responsible and who is not. It's more than that. It's about "where the buck stops."

In the SEAL Teams, when you are in charge, you are accountable for everyone in your care, no matter who did what. You will stand on the carpet and "answer to the man." Accountability is a way of stopping the blame game when things go wrong. Making excuses is not tolerated at any level because it slows down the organization.

115

> A lack of accountability leads to excuses, and
> excuses slow down the organization.

Accountable, but Not Responsible?

To some people, it doesn't seem fair that a person who is not responsible for the mistake can be held accountable. But if you and your organization choose this way of life as leaders and embrace it, you understand and accept the associated risks. Leadership is holistic. It is not just a set of responsibilities. When you're accountable, you become very innovative with respect to the cause-and-effect relationships of all aspects of your team. It's not one thing you do. It's everything you do.

We shape this mindset from day one of BUD/S training. Students are challenged all day, every day, so they experience the ethos that we live by. We give them seemingly impossible tasks and hold them accountable for those tasks.

When we ask them if they completed those tasks, we allow only three responses: "Yes," "No," and "I f***ed up!" Their excuses will not be heard. What we are doing is forcing them to have extreme ownership of the outcome. Making excuses is defensive thinking and will not help us accomplish the mission. It gets in the way of finding the solution. We give them a swift physical remediation and make them move on. We don't let them dwell on failures. Instead, they dust themselves off and tackle the next task.

When you're accountable, "ya got what ya got" and you make the most of it. It's a vital part of the First, Fast, Fearless mindset.

Operating in a Command Climate

In the SEAL world, if a unit is failing the mission, destroying equipment, or having safety mishaps, then the leader is not doing something right. We might not know exactly what he is doing wrong, but we know he's not doing something right. He's not setting the right conditions or what we call the right "command climate"; therefore, he's called to the carpet.

To hold people accountable, we must give people authority to act. We cannot separate the two; we cannot hold people accountable if they do not have authority to make decisions that guide their team's results. This is often the problem with organizations trying to hold people accountable; they don't give their people authority to make decisions that influence the outcomes. When authority is given, so is the trust in leaders to do the right thing as guided by their ethos.

> **Accountability and authority must travel together.**

The command climate does not give your boss carte blanche to hold you accountable when he or she does not give you the resources to accomplish your objectives. Leaders should confront their bosses with the shortfalls they have prior to taking command of a situation, to give them a clear understanding of the risks associated with the lack of resources, manning, training, or other deficiency.

Accountability and the Chain of Command

In 2009, General Stanley McChrystal, who was in charge of all U.S. and NATO forces in Afghanistan, laid out a plan for the "way ahead" for the war. He asked for additional troops to meet the requirements placed upon him by the Commander in Chief. He made it clear what the risks would be if the troop levels were lower than his strategic assessment. Such decisions are made all the time; leaders of leaders are also accountable for accepting the risks that come with not supplying the necessary resources. Accountability goes both up and down the chain of command.

When I showed up at SEAL Team 2 in 2005, the Iraq War was at its peak. It seemed that everyone who could carry a gun was off to war. The mission was changing constantly, and the need for forces was greater than what we had. We had already outstretched our equipment and manning. Unlike the Army and Marines; the Navy is not suited for sustained ground warfare; we normally ride ships!

Making the Most of What You Have

With the high volume of combat in 2005 and with the heavier tactical requirements placed on Commanders, I was given a special promotion from Lieutenant to Lieutenant Commander, to command a Task Unit by the Captain in charge of all East Coast SEAL Teams. To the best of my knowledge, this was the first time this had happened in SEAL Team history.

The Commanding Officer of SEAL Team 2 briefed me. He told me that he knew what a difficult task I had at hand. He understood that I was being dealt a large hand of VUCA and assured me that the SEAL Team community had chosen me, trusting that I had the skills, experience, leadership, and proven track record to figure it out. I appreciated the trust of the community, but the volatility of the situation was extreme. We were heading to the most dangerous place on earth at the tipping point of the war. The uncertainty of the mission and not having the necessary manning, training, and equipment for it ratcheted up the anxiety.

This took place on the heels of the disastrous Operation Red Wings, which was portrayed in the book and movie *Lone Survivor*. The Commander who was killed was a friend of mine. I was sitting at his desk when it happened, and I had to clear out his personal belongings. This was the biggest loss of life in the SEAL Teams since 9/11; it resonates hard throughout the community. The memorial was unlike anything any of us had ever seen. Thousands saw the families of the fallen ripped by grief, and we watched young children receive their dead fathers' medals. The gravity of the situation weighed heavily on me.

I met with the leaders of SEAL Team 2, whom I would command. The SEAL troop had been training together for a year or so before I joined them as a new Task Unit Commanding Officer. We were scheduled to deploy in a couple of months. Not only did we not have much time to get ready but I also realized that the team was way behind. We had no manning for support personnel other than the few who were organic to the team.

I pored over an Excel spreadsheet, pulling the names of about 75 support personnel with different skill sets, none of whom I knew or had met before. The halls of the building were lined with equipment stacked head high for all the Task Units to take with them; it was absolute mayhem. The missions were changing so rapidly that the system could barely keep up.

A SEAL deployment requires a lot more support personnel than it does actual SEALs. You have to have "beans, bullets, and bombs" and find the enemy. All functions need to operate independently in a war zone. All support personnel have to come from the regular Navy, and even in war, it isn't easy to pull people with specialized skills away from a Navy force already stretched thin. Also, Navy sailors don't have combat skills, such as weapons training, running convoys, or survival tactics. We have to put them through a simplified training program quickly to get them to a minimum soldier standard.

My last meeting with my Commanding Officer was right before we left for deployment. We discussed what we would be doing, and I made our shortfalls clear. When you are held accountable, your duty is to be straightforward and clear about the risks imposed by a lack of support. You must have the courage to be honest with your boss, and he must have the courage to hear it.

One was the lack of a tactical local area network (TACLAN) communications system. This critical piece of equipment controls all communications, and it runs all of our secret IT equipment. There were simply no TACLANs in the country that weren't already being used, so we had to work around it. We had to count on the innovation and creativity of our Communicators and IT personnel to make it happen.

The situation was not pretty. I didn't know my team, they didn't know me, and none of us had worked together before. Worse, we didn't have a clearly stated mission.

The last blow before we departed was news that we didn't yet have the funding to build the camp we needed to live in there! (Little did I know at the time that the $1.4 million allocated wouldn't make it to us until we were already back in the States.) We had to get creative. I remember thinking that when history is written, it won't remember my excuses!

> **History won't remember your excuses.**

There Are No Bad Staffs, Just Bad Leaders

The last bit of guidance I received from the Commanding Officer before I deployed went something like this: "Ya got what ya got. Take care of your men, and make it happen." I understood accountability and that leaders don't whine and moan about the hand they are dealt. Leaders who pass the buck or blame their staffs for being inadequate are the problem, not the solution; there are no bad staffs, just bad leaders. If you as a leader do not accept accountability, when your team gets wind of this behavior—and they will—you will set the conditions for theirs.

This behavior, so common among politicians who blame the previous administration or other party, is toxic. In a system in which accountability is the standard, it is unacceptable to whine and pass blame. It doesn't change the situation. Once you accept the cold hard facts of the situation and stop wishing and wanting, you can start to deal with the problem at hand. Put your energy into the solution.

> **Blame is much like fear: it is highly contagious.**

This doesn't excuse your leaders from not giving you the necessary people, resources, or training that you need because they are accountable as well. I made the situation very clear to my boss, but after that, there was nothing to do except throw everything I had at the problem.

When we landed in Ramadi, it was the most dangerous place on earth. There were constant mortar and rocket attacks. There was no safety "behind the lines." Everything and everyone was in reach of a surprise mortar, rocket, or small arms attack. Soldiers were being killed and wounded just coming in and out of the dining facility.

Simple things didn't exist, such as plywood for structures in which to fix vehicles and protect them from the harsh sun and desert dust, and we didn't have the funding for materials to improvise. Vehicles and the weapon systems on them are parts of your life support equipment; they must not fail in time of need. We had money for operational activities, such as gathering intelligence, conducting civil affairs, and other functions, but nothing for building the physical infrastructure of a functioning camp where people can eat, sleep, and bathe.

Chess Players Figure It Out

I brought together all of my support personnel in charge of building infrastructure for what I called a "come to Jesus" meeting. I explained in full what the situation was and what I wished them to do. Our headquarters was assured that we would be getting the line of funding soon so that we could start to build a camp. I knew that this hope and promise might fail because I was fighting the bureaucratic beast.

Among my support personnel, I sought out the one key innovator I felt could get as creative as necessary to acquire what we needed. D.D., as I'll refer to him, became a creative acquisition specialist of the highest quality. He knew what we needed, and I let him know that I had his back to make it happen. My mantra to him was this: you bring it, and I'll sign it. We got very good at getting what we needed to accomplish the mission. We may have bent some rules, but we didn't break them! Mission first.

> **We bend rules. We don't break them.**
> **Mission first.**

Getting around the fortified base in Ramadi required vehicles. To meet with our Iraqi counterparts and the conventional military, we had to drive a mile or so on the base, and we didn't want to use combat vehicles. We acquired some standard vehicles, but we needed more for everyday business for the support personnel. I'll never forget when one of my acquisition specialists worked out a deal with an Iraqi Colonel for a vehicle. NATO had sent him a new Range Rover ambulance with the plastic still on the seats. Ramadi was an extremely dangerous place, with constant IED attacks, so you didn't drive off the base in an unarmored vehicle. It was useless to him. The Colonel had kids, so we traded four soccer balls for the Range Rover and made it our meal truck.

People will figure out a solution if you lead them.

When you know you're accountable, you accept your job in a holistic manner. You don't waste time or energy thinking about how you have been dealt a bad hand. You don't sit around feeling sorry for yourself. You take an offensive, first strike mindset with the reality of your situation. Leaders are never victims. SEALs "thrive in adversity."

In the business world, most of us don't have to worry about mortar attacks on the way to the lunchroom. But in the enterprise, as in combat, you're dealt a hand, and you are—or should be—accountable for executing a mission. The tentacles of bureaucracy will envelop you if you sit back and play the blame game for everything that goes wrong or everything you don't have. First, Fast, Fearless leaders take the offensive mindset, bend the rules prudently, and make it happen with what they have.

Ya got what ya got. Now do something with it!

TAKEAWAYS

- We all operate in a world of change. You can complain about it, or you can take the "ya got what ya got" mentality and move forward. It's all part of the first strike mindset.

- Don't sit around waiting to be dealt a better hand.

- Accountability is greater than responsibility; responsibility still allows you to blame someone or something else for failure.

- Accountability, authority, and trust go together. Don't make people accountable without giving them authority and trusting them to use it.

- History won't remember excuses.

- Do not let your organization be driven by excuses, alibis, or blame. These are contagious and toxic to your organization, and they lead to more bureaucracy.

- Honesty and accountability will get your mission accomplished.

PART II

RUNNING TO THE SOUND OF GUNFIRE

The Essence of Brotherhood

There is no hunting like the hunting of man, and those who have hunted armed men long enough and like it, never care for anything else thereafter.

—ERNEST HEMINGWAY

Little good comes from war. But one good that does is the bonds of brotherhood formed during war's extremes. Is that teamwork? Teamwork and brotherhood are similar but not the same. Brotherhood is much deeper and stronger than teamwork. Brotherhood is a full commitment and promise from each team member to look after each other and to put the well-being of others before themselves.

The Hemingway quote above resonates with the SEAL Teams and similar military units. We don't necessarily miss the dangers and thrills of battle. What we all miss is the intensity of our bonds with one another; we miss the brotherhood.

What forms these bonds? How can we go from high-performing teams to unstoppable brotherhoods that perform and flourish even in the worst of times?

The answers are herein.

CHAPTER 9

The Guiding Light:
Values and Shared Vision

In the spring of 2006, we were deeply involved in a counterinsurgency operation in Iraq, what we call "irregular warfare." Gaining the favor of the civilian population is one of the key tasks in such operations. Typically, during insurgencies, all infrastructure breaks down. Consequently, the basic survival needs of the civilian population must be met. If we didn't meet them, the enemy would—and were at the time. We were competing with the enemy to win the hearts and minds of the people.

The culture in the Al Anbar Province has been tribal for as long as people have lived there. Al Ramadi, the capital, was home to numerous tribes with various levels of power and influence that had been fighting each other for centuries before we came. The dynamics were complex and confusing; it was hard to know the cause and effect you would have when engaging tribal leaders.

But we had to prove to the population that we were there to make things better and to get the country running again. To help establish this "proof," all forces did community projects, such as building wells, bridges, schools, and medical clinics. Providing medical treatment or care to children is a good way to make friends worldwide. Besides winning favor with the local population, it creates new friends who are instrumental to finding the enemy hiding among the civilians.

We were building a well for a tribe that needed water for its community. At the same time, we were building an Iraqi army, one that very much needed to get out in the community and make its presence known. The Iraqi Colonel and I discussed the situation and decided that he would need to be the face of this project. He would have to build a relationship with the tribal leaders in his battle space. It was critical for the Colonel to show that he, not the Americans, was doing this for the local tribe.

The funding for the project came with some rules. The person who brought the money to us was a 26-year-old, blonde, blue-eyed female Lieutenant, who, a week earlier, had been on a ship in the Gulf.

This Lieutenant was a recent Naval Academy graduate and had learned to live by strict unbendable rules of authority. According to the rules governing the funding, she had to physically hand the money to the tribal leader. These rules did not allow for any discretion.

When she arrived at my command, I explained to her that in this culture, it was an insult for a female to be the power broker with a tribal elder. In traditional Arab culture, tribal elders don't do business with women. That's not part of our belief system, but that's not the point. I also explained that we needed the Iraqi Colonel to start to build respect in the community.

Another complication: this Lieutenant had virtually no combat skills training, and she would have been a hindrance if we had been ambushed on our way in or out of the village. I explained to her that I could escort this money and that I would ensure that it got to the right people. To me, it was ironic that I had to convince this Lieutenant—new to war—that I could be trusted to ensure the money got to where it was intended. I thought back to an earlier time in Baghdad when I had wads of money stuffed in cargo pockets, so I could pay informants to help hunt America's high value targets (HVTs). I have the highest security clearance a person can have, and I can be trusted with America's secrets, so it was a little strange having to convince a new Lieutenant that I was trustworthy.

She insisted that the rules mandated that she physically see the money handed to the tribal elder. I assured her that the intent of those rules was to keep her accountable. The mission was more important than a set of rules developed in peacetime by someone who didn't foresee this scenario. The rules would actually hurt the mission, and that was not going to happen.

In the end we figured it out—and did the right thing.

The obvious conflict here was over a set of rules developed in the context of peaceful circumstances and American culture that would not apply in a complex, urgent, unconventional war occurring in a vastly different cultural context. So according to what rules or guidelines do we operate? How do we make the best decisions and move forward?

When navigating in the fog of war and in the world of VUCA, our ethos is our compass. Our values—not the rules—define who we are.

The Great Divide: Values Versus Rules

The point I'm making here is simple: there can never be enough rules or policies to cover every scenario you might possibly face. We train to develop specific skill sets that can be used in any situation, but an ethos-based system provides the real guiding light. Organizations and leaders that live by an ethos are better suited and more adaptable than those that live by the rules alone.

You cannot move at the speed of war when you are caught up in the rules of bureaucracy. Micromanagers often lead with rules; in contrast, organizations that lead with ethos-based leadership can make hard decisions in times of adversity and uncertainty. Ethos matters, and ethos works, especially when accompanied by trust.

> **You cannot move at the speed of war when you are caught up in the rules of bureaucracy.**

Furthermore, there is no rulebook for innovation and creativity, and if there were, it would be obsolete instantly. If you have trustworthy people, and those people can clearly see what an ethical leader and decision maker you are, then you can get the right things done and get them done quickly and efficiently. Of course we need *some* rules, but too many takes discretion away from leaders. They also destroy the ability to change the situation in real time for the success of the mission.

> **There is no rule book for innovation and creativity. If there were, it would be obsolete instantly.**

Managing Versus Leading: The Nickel-and-Dime Effect

People ask me all the time what the true difference is between managing and leading. Simply put, the difference is this: you manage things; you *lead* people. Managing people instead of leading them often results in what I call the "nickel-and-dime effect."

The managers start to see—and look for—trivial faults and mistakes. They focus on things that don't matter to the successful outcome of the mission. Their people are worn out by the sense that these trivial negatives are now the main topic or currency of their relationship with their manager. People resent being managed, but they appreciate and respect being led.

Provide the motivation—and the means—to do something important. Don't micromanage.

> You manage things, but you lead people.

Lubricating an Organization with Values-Based Leadership

Garry Ridge, a friend of mine and fellow University of San Diego Executive Leadership program graduate, is also the CEO of the WD-40 Company. He gives us a fine example of how great organizations can get better with a values-based system.

Garry became president and CEO of WD-40 in 1997. The company had been making consistent profits for more than 40 years. The company's culture was conservative. The company executives figured if it ain't broke, don't fix it.

But Garry didn't see it that way. He thought the company could do more. He knew that to expand the business, he himself would have to grow and learn. He realized that he didn't know as much as he should about leading and the effects of leadership on organizations. Garry took an offensive first strike mindset. He enrolled in the master's program for executive leadership.

You Must Be Bold to Change a Culture

Garry was at the top of his game, yet he had the humility to admit that for the company to realize its potential, he needed to change and grow himself as a leader. He didn't make small rudder corrections; he made First, Fast, Fearless bold changes to the way the company operated.

His first change was to revise the performance review system, a step that effectively changes the culture of an organization. This exercise at WD-40 resembled what we experienced in the SEAL Teams when we created our ethos.

From Silos to Tribes

Garry started to build a "tribal" work environment to encourage teamwork and the sharing of information from existing organizational silos. He used the tribe metaphor, recognizing that tribes have much of what he was looking for in an ethos- and values-based system: identity of belonging, folklore, warriors, individual meaningful work, ceremonies, a constant evolution, a set of norms, and even a unique culture of dress, language, and other customs.

Does this sound familiar? It should, because these elements are characteristic of the SEAL Ethos and tribe.

Vision Is Where You're Going; Your Ethos Gets You There

Forming a tribe doesn't do much good unless you have a central purpose, or overarching mission, for that tribe. Garry knew that he had to clarify the company's vision and values in order to hold people accountable for them. Fear-based bottom-line leadership rooted in greed and rules won't give you the staying power to do the right thing in times of VUCA and stress. Vision is where you are going, and the ethos is what gets you there.

We are part of organizations that have stated values. But how you *live* your values, as individuals and teams, is what is really important.

Here are the stated values of WD-40:

1. Do the right thing.

2. Create positive, lasting memories in all our relationships.

3. Make it better than it is today.

4. Succeed as a team while excelling as individuals.

5. Own it and passionately act on it.

6. Sustain the WD-40 economy (meaning: be profitable).

These values are simple and, notably, not about specific business goals or measures. Garry led the creation of these values, but he involved his teams in dialogue to establish them and ingrain them into the organization as an ethos.

They are not a set of rules; they are a set of guiding moral principles. Like the SEAL Ethos, it is written down. And just like our ethos, it is the standard by which to measure performance and individual achievement. Our *five pillars of leadership* (which hold the leader to be a moralist, jurist, teacher, steward, and philosopher) are used as an evaluative standard in the SEAL Teams.

Using Values to Guide and Measure Performance

How does this look in the real world? I recently consulted with a multi-billion-dollar energy company that wanted to fuse the organization together and get rid of its silos.

The goal was to get the 20-plus parts of the company to act as a team working toward a common mission, rather than just the goals or mission of the individual departments. One of the challenges: the resources of any given team are finite. This led siloed departments to cannibalize other departments to achieve their goals. The effect was detrimental to customers, both internal and external. Does this sound familiar?

My advice was to create a values-based system by which people are evaluated and held accountable for qualities such as teamwork, fairness, and so forth, rather than department or functional performance measures. I suggested using the five pillars of leadership the SEALs use. The system becomes not only one of evaluation but also one of daily operation. As an example from my own world, when my subordinates bring a problem to me as the *steward* of the mission and my people, I review their suggested solutions with my *philosopher* hat on. My policy is, Don't go to a leader with a problem unless you have a solution. As a *moralist*, I figure out which one is fair and which one isn't.

Evaluate the Mission; the Goals Will Take Care of Themselves

I have found that if you guide and measure people according to values, the specific goals and metrics of the organization tend to take care of themselves. That is, if people on your team are acting according to their values and are guided by the big-picture elements of the mission, the specific measures and goals tend to fall in line naturally.

This is particularly important—and often overlooked in the business world. If you and your team members take care of your customers, treat others with respect, "own it and act passionately on it," and do what's right for the profitability of the business, you will likely come out ahead. Sales, costs, profits, customer retention rates—they will all take care of themselves. The values and mission guide the right behaviors. This is the essence of what Garry Ridge brought to WD-40.

> If you have the right values and mission, the goals and metrics tend to take care of themselves.

Wanna Be a Winning Investor?
Embrace the Future, Not the Past.

Stock investors have come up with a thousand ways to analyze financial statements and past performance to winnow out the winners from among the thousands of investments out there. Who has the strongest profits, earnings per share, margins, sales growth, asset and debt ratios, and so forth. This is OK—even good—as far as it goes.

Why only as far as it goes? Mainly because (1) it looks at the past and (2) it looks at only measurable goals. Want a better formula? Look at companies with strong *intangibles*— such as brand, market share, customer mindshare, products, and management. These are indicators of *future*—not past— success. These are companies that have their values and missions right and aren't focused on the past or on short-term goals. With this in mind, some of us might have bought Apple stock in 2004 at a split-adjusted price of $2!

Again, get the values and mission right, and the goals and metrics tend to take care of themselves.

Another example of values-based leadership comes from my mother-in-law, who has been a preschool teacher since Moby Dick was a minnow (or more accurately, a calf). She had a simple way of teaching kids how to be fair and share. She would take a cookie and let one kid cut it and the other kid choose which piece he or she wanted. These kids were only four or five years old, but guess what? The one cutting the cookie always got it right.

In a multi-billion-dollar company, it's a little more complicated to figure out how the cookie is cut but, as a *jurist*, you as a leader have to decide, and if you are truly living an ethos of teamwork, you will decide based on how well they played together and hold them accountable. If the cookie is cut in a lopsided fashion and the person who cut it wants to choose his or her portion first, then you have someone who isn't being a team player. As a leader, reward the team player, and then put on your *teacher* hat and have a leadership moment with the other one.

Garry did just that—and did it according to all of his stated values—in his employees' performance reviews.

> **Be driven by values and missions, not goals.**

Implementing a Values-Based Leadership System

We all want results, and the proof is in the pudding. Since Garry implemented his new performance review system and WD-40 began to live its stated values, the company has been thriving. In the 11 years since he took over, annual sales—in a business most would describe as flat—more than tripled from $100 million in 1997, with only 30 percent from domestic sales, to more than $339 million in 2008, with a healthier 47 percent from domestic sales.

Garry is a great example of a values-driven leader and how that type of leadership can work for any organization with the courage to change. Read the SEAL Ethos and think about what it can do for you and your organization. It's only 440 words, but it has a direct and measurable impact on our nation's most sensitive missions and, ultimately, democracy in the free world. If it can do that, I hope you can trust what our ethos can do for your organization. Use it to guide you and your teams. Make your own leadership ethos, share it with your people, and hold yourself and them accountable.

Being guided by your values is the essence of First, Fast, Fearless leadership.

TAKEAWAYS

- Values and rules are both important. Rules won't—and can't—cover everything. Values help guide what happens in the gray areas between the rules.

- You cannot move at the speed of war when you are caught up in the rules of bureaucracy.

- There is no rule book for innovation and creativity. Having too many rules compromises the ability to adapt to the situation, and ultimately it leaves the organization paralyzed.

- Don't micromanage your people. Micromanaging polarizes the leader and the team. Lead them.

- Values-based leadership is the most effective basis of a performance evaluation. It is a handy tool to overcome organizational silos because it guides action toward a greater good, or *mission*.

- Stated values should be succinct and clear but not too simple; they must tell you what's really expected.

- If you have the right values and mission in place—and evaluate your people according to them—the goals and metrics often take care of themselves.

CHAPTER 10

Powering Teams Forward with TRUST

Spring 2004. It was pitch dark at 0159. I was working with the British Special Forces at the time, and the unit I was with in downtown Baghdad was set to assault a known high value target (HVT) compound just on the perimeter of Sadr City. A district of Baghdad, the Shiites named it after the deceased cleric Mohammad Mohammad Sadeq al-Sadr after the overthrow of Saddam Hussein's regime. Sadr City was an exceptionally dangerous world of its own; moving through it, you knew the chances of contact with the enemy were extremely high.

On this particular night, the assault involved helicopters from a classified Aviation Task Force that works exclusively with Special Forces. The Night Stalkers, as they are called, are the best in the world at flying in such operations. Having worked with them over the years, I've built up a lot of respect and trust in their ability to do what they say they will do.

We snuck through the city and placed a large explosive charge on the front gate of an enemy compound.

At 0200 the helicopters would arrive as we blew the gate off the compound and stormed the first floor of the building. The helicopter team was flying our second assault force in to "fast rope" onto the building. To fast rope onto a targeted building, a large 1.6-inch-diameter rope is pushed out of the helicopter. Once it hits the roof, the assault force slides down the rope quickly as the pilot hovers. A 10-man assault force can get down the rope in a matter of seconds. Coordination is critical for us to maintain the assault elements of surprise, speed, and violence of action.

At exactly 0200, we blew the gate. Simultaneously, the helicopters appeared overhead to insert the second assault team. The whole takedown took only minutes to clear the entire structure. The mission depended on the coordination and trust between two units from two different countries.

What is "team trust," and how do you build it? Bottom line up front: without trust, there is *no* team, just a bunch of individuals looking out for themselves. A lack of trust leads to micromanagement, bureaucracy, paranoia, rules-based management, resentment, dishonesty, and a host of other organizational ills.

How does an organization build the sort of trust I wrote about in my story? Trust upon which we would risk our lives? Over the years, I've found what great teams do to build trust in a variety of environments, from the battlefield to the boardroom. They share common themes and principles:

- **T**ime and attention
- **R**espect
- **U**nbreakable values
- **S**acrifice
- **T**echnical proficiency

Time and Attention

We are all born with time in our life bank account, if you will. Your attention is how you spend it. These are limited resources.

When I was in graduate school, I heard many classmates complain about how much of their day was being wasted in meetings without a clear agenda or purpose. (I'm sure you can relate!) They all resented their bosses' apparent disregard for their time.

Time Waits for No One

When you are in charge, you must pay close attention to how you use other people's time. When you hold meetings, you must be prepared and on time.

In the first week of BUD/S training, we learned a hard lesson about how important being on time is to establishing trust. We were constantly given too much to do and not enough time to do it (sound familiar?). We learned that although we are busy, we must be on time and reliable to the team:

> On one particular morning, we had to stage equipment after our morning workout. We were running a little behind schedule. It was almost time to be at our next event at the Combat Training Tank (CTT), a huge pool in which we teach water skills.
>
> The Combat Training Tank is over a mile away from our normal facility. Before we went there, we needed to get the class through the line to eat. We decided not to rush our breakfast, and we showed up significantly late to the CTT for training—and were met by one of the meanest and most intimidating instructors we had. Chief Jako was muscular, with a shaved head, dark wraparound sunglasses, and a colorful vocabulary.
>
> When we arrived and formed up to receive our briefing, Chief Jako was standing on the 10-meter dive platform and said only one thing: "Eight count body builders—begin!"

Starting from a standing position, you squat down, hands on the deck, push your legs into the pushup position, do a down-and-up pushup, spread your legs and put them back together, put your feet back into the squat position, and then stand up. We all hate eight count body builders. That day we did eight count body builders from the time we got there until it was time for lunch.

All we had on were shorts. The entire surface is rough concrete. By the time we were done, most students' feet were bleeding. The only breaks we took were to hydrate. Once Chief Jako secured us, he went to the class leader and said, "Don't be late," and he walked off. I don't remember our class ever being late again.

Time matters when you are on a team, whether you are leading or following. Be on time and prepared for meetings, make timely decisions, submit timely reports, communicate on time, respect other people's time, and be reliable.

When you are in charge, it matters even more. "The boss is never late" is an old saying that we use sarcastically, meaning that he is in charge and we are therefore on his schedule. In reality, nothing could be further from the truth because every minute the boss is late, he steals a minute from each person waiting.

Leaders don't allow this to happen, and if they do, an authentic apology is due. All we have in life is in our bank account of time. Every day, it decreases, and we don't collect interest! The ability to manage time is a critical part of leadership and of building team trust.

On Time, On Target

Before one of my most difficult deployments, I was having some doubts and needed someone to be a "swim buddy." But being in charge, I knew that expressing my fears and doubts to anyone on the team was unacceptable. I called my best friend,

Matt, to talk; he could hear it in my voice. He dropped what he was doing and said he'd be there the next day. It was too late that day for him to get a plane ticket, so he jumped in his truck and drove a thousand miles so he could be there when he said he would. I trusted that he'd be there, and he was. Matt was a career helicopter pilot. He was on time and on target.

> Their time is just as important—if not more so—than yours.

Timely Decisions Versus Untimely Indecisions

Over the years I have found that people who tend not to respect time—theirs or others'—tend also to be indecisive. Insensitivity to time reduces urgency and leads to procrastination. You can see how these two effects could be disastrous to a SEAL Team operation. More subtly, they can degrade the performance and reduce the morale of your enterprise. As philosopher and psychologist William James put it, "There is no more miserable human being than one in whom nothing is habitual but indecision."

Be timely, and respect the time of others; it is part of the First, Fast, Fearless mindset.

Respect: A Two-Way Street

Leaders set the climate for the behavior of their team much the way parents set the behavior for their children. If parents are explosive and tend to escalate emotions with irrational behavior, their children tend to do the same. We have an expression in the SEAL Teams: "Your personality is like herpes—it truly flares during times of stress." It's easy to be respectful to everyone when things are going well and you are in a good state of mind, but when it's not going well, it isn't so easy. Respect needs to be genuine and continuous; it is a perpetual state of mind and being.

In every leadership position I've held, I've had a policy that the team was like a family, all of whom would be held accountable for respecting each other equally. I posted rules that reflected this model of trust. It's very easy to forget that the person who answers the phone is entitled to the same respect as the senior leader; both are human beings. Respect the janitor as much as the CEO.

Most people shake their head as if to say, "Of course." But it doesn't always happen in practice. The key to success is to live by it and to hold other team members accountable.

Respect Means Not Getting Too Caught Up in Power

From day one of SEAL training, we're taught to live by the phrase, "Nobody cares about you as much as you do." Although we are a team that looks after each other and a team that has safety mechanisms built into everything we do, at the end of the day, you have to look after your own life. Everyone views life through his own eyes and values his own life. Remember, in a position of authority and power, it becomes far too easy to become delusional with your own self-worth. That power and position can make you disrespectful, even mean.

It's not uncommon for leaders to treat their boss one way and their subordinates another. Respecting and caring about people on the team equally helps to form bonds, and teams that bond perform better. In a position of authority, it's very easy to fall into the trap of using fear to get respect. That isn't *earned* respect; in fact, it isn't really respect. It's not real because when your position goes, so does the respect you think you had from your people.

> Gain respect the old-fashioned way. *Earn it.*
> Never resort to fear.

Respecting People's Talents Builds Trust

One of the things that I have recognized about the SEALs I've led is that everyone has *dominant talents* or abilities he holds dear. These talents become a strong base for respect and, ultimately, trust. I've always felt that mine is the ability to take complex issues with large amounts of information and make sense of them with a clear and simple plan. I wasn't the smartest, the strongest, or even the best operator, but I could always figure out the tough things.

In positions where that talent was stifled and unrecognized, I felt disgruntled and unappreciated. I learned a lot from how I felt and used that wisdom to guide how I treated my people. I made a point to identify each man's dominant talent—that is, the skill or ability he felt most proud of. It wasn't necessarily the talent that I saw; it was the talent *he* saw. Sometimes they were one and the same, but sometimes they weren't.

I made a point to always recognize that talent when it came up in their work. I know people love to do what they are good at, so good leaders let them do it. If a SEAL was what we call a "sky god" and knew everything about air operations, I would compliment him and task him with more jobs in that field. I would always refer to him as a "sky god"; that made him want to be more of an expert. It showed my respect and trust in him, and that only deepened his respect and trust in me.

> **Find the dominant talents.**
> **Turn them into respect and trust.**

*Un*breakable Values:
Keeping the Compass Aligned

When a loved one asks, "Does this dress make me look fat?" we are thrust into a conflict of values. Of course, honesty and telling the truth are important, but so are the feelings of the people whom you care about! Every day, our values are being tested, and often, they are in competition with one another. That makes it more important than ever to live by an ethos instead of a set of rules.

If You Ain't Cheatin', You Ain't Tryin'

"If you ain't cheatin', you ain't tryin'" is a common phrase used in BUD/S training. This statement has been debated for years—and probably always will be. It was discussed a great deal at our off-site ethos conference.

Bending the rules is a slippery slope requiring constant attention in any innovative organization. Moral issues are often not black and white; they require the leader to step back and base actions on the stated ethos. Most organizations don't have a stated ethos, so the outcome of moral decisions can vary greatly. In war, right and wrong vary by a matter of degrees; black-and-white answers are hard to find. We always keep in mind that the mission is the destination and the ethos is how we get there; this provides moral guidance in VUCA.

> Without an ethos, the outcome of moral decisions can vary greatly.

They Don't Recruit Navy SEALs from Choir Practice

SEALs and other Special Forces are rule benders. Put bluntly, "do-gooders" don't do well in Special Forces.

People like the young Lieutenant at the beginning of Chapter 9 frequently have a rigid definition of their values. However, VUCA environments require leaders to rely on their *moralist* and *philosopher* pillars to do the right thing. I bent the rules as a Task Unit Commander, but I know I did the right thing. And I was willing to explain to my Commanding Officer why I did what I did. That's the test.

If you're still not sure you're doing the right thing, here's another test. Ask yourself, "Does what I'm doing or what I've decided support the mission as a whole? And not just from my vantage point?" Would you save the victims of an auto crash even if it were "against the rules"? Servant leaders continually ask themselves whether they are doing the right thing for the mission of the organization and the people. Always err on the side of team values.

> As a leader, you should expect mistakes
> with expertise, knowledge, and experience,
> but values-based mistakes should be dealt
> with swiftly and not allowed.

Far Enough, but Not Too Far

I am not trying to turn you into a perpetual rule bender. Not only can that be disruptive or annoying to those around you but ultimately it can also destroy trust, not create it. As Nietzsche said, "I'm not upset that you lied to me. I'm upset that from now on, I can't believe you."

How does bending the rules gain trust? You must be true to the ethos, true to the team, and true to the situation at hand—that builds trust. Being only "about yourself" destroys trust.

Sacrifice: Putting Their Needs Ahead of Yours

When we first started combat advising and combined operations with the Iraqis in 2005, neither side trusted the other. We knew going in that we needed to build trust and build it fast because in short order, we would be leading and conducting combat operations with our newly formed Iraqi counterparts. We didn't know how many of them we had fought against at the initial start of the war. It's a little unnerving not knowing the true intent of the AK-47-toting armed men behind you.

When we arrived, we took ownership of the situation. We spent our "time and attention" focusing on their basic human needs, such as food, berthing, and pay. They had combat equipment supplied by the United States, but they lived in very poor conditions. They were not getting paid properly and on time, so we sent a tiger team (a couple of people) to route the source of the problem and to get their money. We went to their dining facility and noticed that their food was rancid.

The money coming from Baghdad was being skimmed by every layer of the newly formed government; it was "business as usual." We put a stop to that and got the other two-thirds of the money that had been taken. We had our builders construct adequate berthing. Our acquisition specialist acquired simple comforts, such as blankets and cots for every one of them. They saw that we had their best interests in mind.

When we started conducting missions, we went in the door first. We knew that we couldn't ask them to do something that we weren't willing to do ourselves. We also wanted them to know that we shouldered the same burden of combat that they did. One of my Senior Enlisted Chiefs came up to me early on and mentioned that he didn't think we should be driving around in the sophisticated mine-resistant vehicles if we didn't have enough for the Iraqis. They drove to missions in open flatbed trucks sitting on sandbags and makeshift steel sides, without much protection from enemy fire or IEDs. He didn't want the Iraqis to see us driving around in our armored vehicles because it showed that we didn't truly respect their lives. It showed that we weren't willing to sacrifice as much as we were asking them to. Initially, I didn't like the idea, but I agreed. Building trust quickly was part of the mission; we all had to take risks.

The willingness to sacrifice is one of the "secret sauces" of building trust. Sacrifice provokes a strong emotion, and people respond. That sacrifice—and assorted smaller sacrifices among teammates—served to build trust.

> **Sacrifice as much as or more than you expect of your teams.**

Technical Proficiency: Knowing How to Get It Done

We have an expression: "It takes a shooter to lead a shooter." This is drilled into every new officer coming into the SEAL Teams. It's really simple: You must not only be a good leader. You must also be a good *operator*.

We refer to an operator as a person who is technically and tactically proficient at the individual skills of warfare. As a SEAL, you are expected to be a lifelong learner of your chosen profession. Each SEAL returning from a deployment starts six months of professional development. That training includes new skills, such as sniper training, language training, emergency medical training, and a selection of professional education courses that include philosophy, leadership, history, and warfare. As our SEAL Ethos states, "My training is never complete." SEALs are constantly developing to prepare themselves for the duties of greater responsibility.

Thinking Men and Fighting Men Are One and the Same— Don't Mess with That

Due to our overt role as leaders, SEAL Officers focus more on professional education than on building individual tactical skills. But we don't draw definitive lines between the officers and the regular SEALs. As the historian and philosopher Thucydides once said:

> The nation that will insist on drawing a broad line of demarcation between the fighting man and the thinking man is liable to find its fighting done by fools and its thinking done by cowards.

Officers are required to pursue professional education and are encouraged to seek graduate-level degrees when the career opportunities arise. We have established relationships with academic institutions, including the Navy Postgraduate School, the University of San Diego, and Princeton University. General David Petreaus, who was credited with turning the tide in Iraq, has a doctorate degree. Great leaders are never ignorant.

There are few honors higher to a SEAL than being referred to as a "great operator." It means that he has mastered the trade skills and leadership skills for his level. Be an operator, and people will trust your performance.

> Do what you expect your teams to do, and know what you expect your teams to know.

Inside Out: Driving External Trust with Team Trust

The British forces under the command of our Joint Special Operations Command (JSOC) knew that they were trustworthy even though they hadn't worked with them before. They knew JSOC wouldn't have a force that wasn't trustworthy; the

U.S. government trusted JSOC from years of experience. Use TRUST to establish trust, and protect it the way you would a brand. That's what First, Fast, Fearless leaders do.

Other people and other teams know that if you can count on each other, they can count on you. The internal trust within your team, department, or organization develops into a trustworthy brand. Consistent internal trust over time leads to trust with an organization's customers.

TAKEAWAYS

- TRUST: time and attention, respect, unbreakable values, sacrifice, and technical proficiency all serve to build trust in you, in each other, and within the greater organization.

- Always be on time, and respect the time of others. Treat their time as more important than yours.

- Missing deadlines—and too much deadline risk—impairs team trust.

- Respect must be honest and continuous.

- Never use fear to gain respect.

- Respect people for their dominant talents.

- Your values will be tested every day. Conflicts will inevitably arise, especially in VUCA. Very few judgments are black and white.

- When it isn't black and white, your core values will guide you.

- Bending the rules in favor of values gains trust, but don't be a perpetual rule bender.

- Don't expect others to do things you wouldn't do yourself. Making sacrifices, large and small, builds trust.

- Do—and be able to do—what you expect your teams to do, and know what they are expected to know. They'll trust you, and you'll trust them.

- Teams that have established trust within themselves build a good reputation outside their teams; it becomes part of their brand.

CHAPTER 11

Two Is One, One Is None: The Power of Swim Buddies

During one BUD/S class, we put one of the slowest students with one of the fastest, whom we nicknamed "Lampshade." Lampshade was an officer. He was a massive man you wouldn't want to meet in a dark alley, yet he could run like a Kenyan and swim like Michael Phelps. The slow student was working through an injury and failed the swim, despite Lampshade's help. The instructor staff logged Lampshade as a failure as well. One more failure could get them both taken to a performance board that would determine if they would remain in SEAL training.

On the next swim, Lampshade put a lanyard of ¼-inch green tubular nylon around himself and his swim buddy to pull him along. It worked. They passed the swim together. But as the instructors pulled up in a kayak, one saw the lanyard and wanted to kick both of them out for a breach of integrity. However, as the leader of the exercise, not only did I not kick them out but I also tore up their deficiency "chits."

I held a long meeting with the instructors; this was a leadership moment. SEALs are very passionate about our ethos and who gets into the brotherhood, so the discussion required all five pillars: *moralist, jurist, teacher, steward*, and *philosopher*. The discussion was about values and how we wanted SEALs to be mission driven, innovative rule benders, not "rule breakers." But here was an affirmation of the idea of a swim buddy, an important concept for the SEAL Teams.

It isn't hard to grasp the idea and importance of having a swim buddy as a companion and an extra pair of eyes in the water. But in practice, this simple idea is the force that transforms lone individuals into strong mini-teams, and those mini-teams into a powerful unit that performs in the face of adversity.

Two people with complementary skills and abilities working together toward a common goal can be more than twice as effective as one man alone. They leverage each other's skills and presence; they cover each other; and they help each other deal more effectively with VUCA. In the SEAL world, we always approach difficult tasks with a swim buddy. Without a swim buddy, the individual not only has no help but he is also more vulnerable.

Swim Buddy—Now and Always

During training, BUD/S students learn the importance of having someone with them during every swim and every "evolution," or training event—through shooting, diving, explosives, hitting the surf, carrying a log, and even when going to see an instructor. Two people can combine strengths, mitigate weaknesses, and expand perception beyond one. We teach new SEALs to never leave a swim buddy alone and to never allow themselves to be left alone. If they are, the remediation is immediate and painful. They can choose any member of the team, which helps build cohesiveness in the teams unmatched by any fighting force in the world.

Swim Buddy Math: Two Is One— and One Plus One Equals Three

"Two is one, one is none" is a mantra for every SEAL. Throughout BUD/S training, you will hear trainees yelling repeatedly, "I need a swim buddy." The idea is imprinted early into their thinking, and it is deeply ingrained by the time they finish BUD/S training.

A SEAL might have to hit the surf for a cold swim because he has screwed up some task, and that means a swim buddy must be willing to hit the surf with him. This is not optional. The cold water is the worst part of training, and although everybody hates it, some of his teammates will volunteer. And the students don't get to dry off when they come out of the water. They are wet and cold until nature dries them.

Swim buddies use their strengths to help teammates, thus helping the entire team. If you have a student who barely passes the timed open-water swims, the class will take one of the fastest swimmers and put him with the slow swimmer. This helps by freeing the slow student from having to navigate in the open water. Navigating requires that you lift your head, which pushes your legs down in the water, and it slows you down. If you don't lift your head, you can zigzag and swim farther than if you swim a straight line. For a slow swimmer, this extra distance can make the difference between passing and failing a swim.

The swim buddy concept accomplishes the larger goal of getting everybody across the finish line faster. The class succeeds because swim buddies use their strengths to help their teammates succeed. But there is much more than combined strength to the swim buddy principle. Most of it is psychological, and every bit of it is tested in the heat of combat during times of VUCA. You make better decisions when someone else is with you. You are braver and stronger, and when held accountable for each other, both of you tend to perform at a higher level. To test this principle yourself, drive alone into the forest on a pitch-black night, stop your car, and turn off the lights. You are probably pretty nervous. Now, get a friend to go with you and do the same thing. The nature of the experience is transformed. You are practically fearless when your friend is with you.

A swim buddy is with you all the time, not just during training. That same person is going through the same missions you are. You are also his swim buddy. We do everything in even numbers, so every man has a swim buddy.

> **Swim buddies get everyone across the finish line faster.**

Through, By, and With: A Shared Accountability

If members of the team are suffering through an evolution, swim buddies step up, take the punishment along with their teammates, and give their struggling teammates a rest. They sacrifice for each other. They do this not as an abstract duty and certainly not to get points with the instructors. They do it because they put the welfare of their teammates ahead of their own, and they put the welfare of the team ahead of everything else.

The instructors reinforce this concept incessantly. If a student shows up for a dive with some problem with his dive rig—a valve not adjusted right, his weight belt backward, not enough air in his tank, missing his "buddy line," a dull knife, or any of dozens of possible oversights—the instructor will point to the student's swim buddy and say, "Drop down." This practice seems callous to outsiders, punishing the one man for the error of the other, but if you focus on the core principle the instructor is reinforcing, you will see how powerful this idea is. It goes back to accountability. If you want teams to be accountable, hold them accountable for each other.

> If you want teams to be accountable,
> hold them accountable for each other.

Teamwork and Camaraderie

Most everything SEALS do in training is aimed at and benefits from intensely close teamwork. This is a lesson in itself. The teams work by virtue of the cohesive, unified structure of their organization. Every man works as part of a team.

All SEALs have found that this feeling of teamwork—the protection of, by, and from your teammates—builds a high level of awareness and trust. Not only is it practical—you always have two sets of eyes and ears—but it builds a spirit of camaraderie that strengthens the team and drives the success of the mission. There is something fundamental about having someone else with you, watching your back, to whom you are loyal and accountable as well.

The act of committing fully to your swim buddy will change you. Your swim buddy will provide a worthwhile goal you can work toward every day. Most people gain a strong sense of accomplishment by helping someone. The desire to help your fellow human beings is a core human trait. The best part of every Navy SEAL—and there are many—is his commitment to the team and to his swim buddy.

Mutual Protection

As a practical matter, in warfare, you don't want to go anywhere alone. You are safer when someone is with you. One watches out for the other. If one gets hurt, the other is there to help.

Your swim buddy's welfare is more important than your own, and vice versa. This is crucial to building teams. A team player will try harder to protect his teammate than he will to protect himself. This is one of the most powerful concepts in the lives of SEALs.

You see to your teammate's survival before you see to your own. That means, of course, that he's doing the same thing. This mutual commitment creates a force between you that is much stronger than either of you would be individually.

Fulfillment of Basic Social Needs

Many professionals talk about close personal relationships as a major component of fulfillment, success, and happiness. People without such close contact and trust become depressed, feel disenfranchised, and may shut down. They feel like they have to go it alone, and they don't succeed. It is in our innate social nature to seek companionship, especially when accomplishing dangerous or difficult tasks. Research has shown that life expectancy is closely tied to your ability to establish close, trusting relationships.

In military life, isolation is an effective way to drive a person insane. The Geneva Convention, which governs the humanitarian laws of war, considers extended isolation to be a form of torture. Humans need other humans. We need swim buddies, even if we don't know it. People live longer and healthier lives when they have swim buddies. Even memories are clearer when they involve other people.

A Little Friendly Competition

You will benefit immensely from working together with someone toward the same goal, sharing new ideas and perspectives. Swim buddy teams are effective because both members strive together for improvement, and they may even engage in a little friendly competition, pushing each other to be the best that they can be. Competition is natural—and a natural incentive to succeed.

> **Most successful people have a swim buddy.**

Swim Buddies in Real Life

Swim buddies are major enablers of the First, Fast, Fearless mindset. Without a swim buddy, fear and anxiety about general safety and the absence of key skills can get in the way of action, especially *successful* action.

How does this apply to life in the real world? How does it apply to life in the organization or enterprise?

In the civilian world, I have found that successful people recognize the swim buddy concept and use it, often without realizing what it is. They may call their swim buddy a "partner," an "associate," or a "teammate." They have a swim buddy to bounce ideas off of, mesh their strengths and weaknesses with, and support them throughout.

Career Companions: Bill and Hillary

Bill and Hillary Clinton offer an excellent example. They worked together, traveled together, and consulted each other on key policy issues and decisions. They covered each other's backs (in a big way during the Monica Lewinsky scandal), and they protected and encouraged each other. He was president for eight years, and she was a U.S. senator and then secretary of state. Together, they have been arguably the most influential husband and wife in the history of American politics.

Whether or not the Clintons consciously decided to be "swim buddies" (I doubt they're familiar with the phrase), they owe much of what they've accomplished to their understanding and application of the swim buddy principle.

The Light Doesn't Shine on Both of Us:
Arnold Schwarzenegger

A slightly different real-life example is actor, bodybuilder, and former California governor Arnold Schwarzenegger. In his book *Arnold: The Education of a Bodybuilder*, he describes how important it was for him to find the right training partner. Schwarzenegger was not particularly gifted as a team player and seemed concerned with only his own personal victories, but his description of the role of the training partner is one of the best ever written.

A swim buddy just needs to be there. He or she does not have to share equally in the recognition and stature. Many a well-known CEO has a less recognized CFO, COO, CMO, or other key player working in tandem with him or her for success. Schwarzenegger was very deliberate and chose the person who would help him become the best bodybuilder in history—but that person is invisible to the outside world.

> **A swim buddy doesn't always share the spotlight. He or she may work in the background.**

Swim Buddies in Organizational Life

In today's business world, it seems to me that very few know the power of swim buddies, although many may have them without realizing it.

People tend to be more isolated and disengaged at work, and they are miserable as a result. In the business world, there is plenty of VUCA, and the resulting anxiety, stress, and uncertainty about outcomes—not to mention your own abilities—can consume you. Nobody has all of the skill sets—technical, personal, experiential—to succeed in every situation. If you can find a swim buddy in the workplace, someone to share your goals with you, to watch your back, to count on you in return, then every aspect of your organizational life will be better. That person can be from the same team, from another department or team, or have a different skill background or skill set.

A swim buddy can watch out for you. She can keep her eyes and ears open when you're not around and tell you what others think of you, or at least what they are saying about you—but she isn't a spy! She advocates for you and knows that your success is also her success. Remember, swim buddies partner with all members of the team.

A Mentor? Not Exactly.

Mentorship has been a popular concept for individuals working in an enterprise, especially for young or new employees entering an organization. Find a senior manager or individual contributor, follow in his or her footsteps, and ask him or her questions informally off the record to learn more about how to advance or how to navigate choppy waters.

It's a good idea, and I don't disagree with it. But that mentor won't have time to watch your back or help you out most of the time. If I'm on a dangerous underwater mission, a mentor back at HQ isn't going to help much. A swim buddy is a peer, someone more like you, facing many of the same issues, with "always-on" availability.

Jobs and Wozniak

The story is now familiar. After brief stints at tech giant Hewlett-Packard, Steve Jobs and Steve Wozniak went off and changed the world. Did they have the same skill sets? Hardly. Jobs was a visionary and a marketing genius. Wozniak had exactly none of those traits. He was (and still is) a technical wizard, providing the technical know-how to create a brilliant product, and he served as Jobs's right-hand man through its development and launch. They collaborated, shared ideas, and assuaged each other's fears in a new and scary world. (Would you have wanted to compete with IBM in the mid-1970s?) Woz was Jobs's swim buddy, and Jobs was Woz's. Without that relationship, the whole Apple story—and perhaps the revolutionary story of personal technology as a whole—would have turned out differently.

Hewlett and Packard: A Success and a Failure

Most of you may be familiar with the business partnership of HP cofounders Bill Hewlett and David Packard. Although both were competent technologists, Bill was more comfortable dealing with the technology and engineering side of things, while Dave tackled business vision and development. They worked together on most projects and made decisions together. It wasn't "Bill" or "Dave"; it was always "Bill and Dave." As I see it, they weren't just partners. They were swim buddies.

That said, latter-day HP offers us an example of a good swim buddy opportunity that *didn't* happen. When HP, led by Carleton "Carly" Fiorina, acquired Compaq Computer in a hotly contested transaction in 2002, everyone thought the combination of her vision, Wall Street savvy, and general leadership skills with Compaq CEO Michael Capellas's operational skills and experience would be tough to beat. They would have made good swim buddies.

However, Fiorina chose the go-it-alone approach. Capellas sensed this and stepped down six months after the acquisition. Through the rest of her tenure, Fiorina chose to go it alone, and she marginalized several other potential swim buddies in the executive ranks. There was no COO, CMO, or CIO in this sprawling, complex organization. Her inability to take on a swim buddy is widely thought to have contributed to her ouster, and it ultimately compromised the performance of the merged company.

Getting Everyone to Buddy Up

I've shown how swim buddies bring together complementary skill sets and provide an extra pair of eyes and ready hands to take on complex or scary tasks. Swim buddies provide extra protection, a sounding board, and a second creative mind to solve any problem. And they don't cost a thing!

> **Swim buddies don't cost a dime.**

Every leader should tap into the power of swim buddies. Create opportunities in your organization for employees to find swim buddies and an environment that promotes this kind of relationship. Make the suggestion. Assign the swim buddy: "Why don't you work with so-and-so in Engineering to see what you can come up with?"

As a leader, *you* can be the swim buddy. Ultimately, if you're really doing things right, eventually swim buddies will self-select and pair up on their own. Until that happens, the message should be: "Don't go it alone." Reward your subordinates for using a swim buddy effectively, especially when they choose one of their own. Hold that up as an example.

If you have swim buddies on your team, hold them jointly accountable for their performance. Their accountability to each other will follow naturally and will strengthen their performance. It's a positive cycle.

Two is one, and one is none. A good swim buddy will help you unlock the other principles in this book—and make you a First, Fast, Fearless leader.

TAKEAWAYS

- Swim buddies provide protection, strengthen teamwork, expand vision, bring together complementary skills, and are accountable to each other.

- People accomplish more with swim buddies. The lone-wolf model can work, but it has many shortcomings.

- Swim buddies create strong mini-teams within a team.

- Swim buddies put the welfare of their buddies and the team before anything else.

- Swim buddies are particularly helpful when dealing with VUCA and adversity.

- Although some may not realize it, most successful people have swim buddies.

- Some swim buddies work in the background and away from the limelight.

- A swim buddy isn't the same thing as a mentor, although a mentor *can be* a swim buddy.

- A well-led team will form swim buddy relationships naturally. Some teams may need encouragement or even direct assignment.

- Swim buddies produce better results and make any team stronger—at no cost.

- First, Fast, Fearless leadership works best with swim buddies. Most SEAL leadership principles *assume* swim buddies within teams.

CHAPTER 12

Through, By, and With: Developing Teamability and Shared Consciousness

When we are "downrange" in the center of combat, we have what we call the Tactical Operations Center (TOC), which is a lifeline for everything that a tactical unit does. Staffed by all types of military specialists, the TOC is designed to track, monitor, and coordinate troops in the field and to pass and receive communications. Its makeup is similar to a mission control center you might see in the movies, with a series of laptops, large-screen monitors, radios, and people working to track the movements of our troops in the field.

Unlike the movies, in combat, the TOC is often in a bombed-out building with work areas compartmentalized by plywood walls with cables snaking down them and desert sand everywhere.

The TOC is the eyes and ears of the battlefield, and it is staffed around the clock with or without troops in the field. You never know when you'll hear an immediate problem you can help solve or when you need to support the other friendly forces in the area. As we say, "One team, one fight."

The TOC always has an Officer in Charge (OIC) to make command-level decisions that affect the whole unit. The TOC itself is led by a Senior Enlisted Advisor (SEA). He manages the progress of the missions, and he leads the staff working on the TOC floor. He makes sure everything is working much as a plant foreman does. Most of the time, the TOC floor is just business as usual: people are tracking, planning, and coordinating normal activities. But when it changes, it changes quickly.

When units are in the field, the TOC monitors everything they do and what is going on around them. We pass information to them to improve their battlefield situational awareness. One event changes the atmosphere more than any other: when the radiomen get the call "Troops in Contact," or "TIC." The SEA in charge of the TOC stands up and yells it loudly: "Troops in Contact!" At this moment, we stop everything we're doing and remain silent until we receive further instructions.

TIC means that our troops are engaged in gunfire with the enemy, so we as teammates are there to help support their needs with everything we have. In our team environment, this moment gives evidence that strong teams can and do have a shared consciousness. Everyone on the team focuses on the problem at hand and how he can contribute to the solution without being told to do so.

One of the most famous TIC events is portrayed in the bestselling book and box-office hit *Lone Survivor*. Four SEALs were compromised deep in enemy territory in Afghanistan and were in a ferocious firefight with an overwhelming Taliban force. In the movie, when the TOC received word of the firefight, they immediately mobilized all troops available as a reactionary force to go in and help fight off the Taliban. The Commanding Officer portrayed in that scene, Lieutenant Commander Erik Kristensen, a good personal friend of mine, led the force into Taliban-held territory. His helicopter was shot down during the insert, and everyone on board was killed.

When teams are strong, they become a brotherhood, and when their teammates are in trouble, teammates run toward the sound of gunfire to help them.

It's about the swim buddy beside you, in front of you, and behind you. It's about being part of a team. It's about being around people you trust who are willing to sacrifice for each other. It's about team.

It's about *teamability*, the ability and willingness to be part of a team, to put the team first, to sacrifice for the team, and to make the team better. It's a visceral thing—you live it. And yes, some of us have died for it.

When people ask me what I miss most about SEAL life, my only true response is, "I miss it *all!*" The life of a SEAL is not as glamorous as the movies might portray. You're uncomfortable most of the time. Your mind and body are frequently pushed to their limits. You face adversity, danger, and fear as a way of life. I'll be the first to tell you that I was never particularly fond of jumping out of airplanes at 30,000 feet, in minus 40-degree temperatures, with over 150 pounds of equipment strapped to my body, only to land in a place on a mission that may end my life. What I miss most is the brotherhood.

Working Backward: Putting Mission Before Me

Every day, SEALS do what I refer to as "working backward," which means we start by taking care of the largest element, working our way to the smallest element—the individual.

Take, for example, an open-water exercise called a "ship attack dive." A ship attack dive might start with a parachute jump, with boats, out of a plane into the open ocean. After we consolidate in the boats, we might transit for miles until we insert and swim to a beach or set point near the harbor, where the ships are docked. Using a rebreather, we dive and swim to the ship, plant an explosive limpet, and swim back to our set point. From there we load up our equipment and then swim back out to sea to rendezvous with our boats to extract. Even if we rehearse only parts of this process, we care for our equipment the same way.

The first thing we do after the dive (besides take our explosives off the ship, seeing as it's an exercise) is to clean and prepare the boats for the entire Task Unit. Then we break into our platoons and maintain all the platoon gear, followed by the squad gear, fire team gear, swim buddy gear, and finally, the individual gear. Only after all the gear is clean do we shower and get something to eat.

The thought process behind this is simple: we might not have time to prepare later, so if something needs to be done, it needs to be done *now*. If we focus on ourselves rather than on the team or the team assets, then the team won't be ready. We can't afford to forget what's important; for us it's a matter of life and death. Our gear maintenance ritual helps to build teams and reinforce teamability.

This is a way of life. We sacrifice individual comforts to address team issues and tasks immediately. All our meetings follow this progression. We deal with team issues first, followed by Task Unit issues and individual issues. We follow this practice as ritual in everything we do. Not only does it keep us prepared but it also serves as a way of reinforcing mission before self.

It Goes Both Ways on Good Teams: Leaders Take a Beating Too

We hold people accountable and show them what accountability means throughout the duration of our training, beginning with BUD/S training and not ending until we leave the SEAL Teams. At all times, a senior ranking person is in charge and is accountable for the team.

We enforce this accountability whether we are at a civilian training facility, at a party, traveling, or anywhere else. Someone is in charge and will be held accountable for the team. We often come together from different SEAL Teams to train for skills or positions such as sniper or range safety officer. When we do, someone is the "senior man" and takes the role of class leader. We expect to lead and to be led.

Inevitably in BUD/S training, the class makes mistakes. The class might be late, or they might not have properly maintained their equipment. They might not have followed specific instructions in loading out weapons or explosives. They might not have properly cleaned their weapons so they could sleep longer!

When such mistakes happen, we take the officers aside for a physical remediation. They hit the surf, do push-ups, run sprints carrying a log in soft sand, or perform other forms of physical activity. We separate the officers from the class, but the class is close enough to see the action and to realize that their officers are taking a beating because of them. It's a significant teaching moment for leaders and team members alike. It reinforces the solidarity of the team.

Now in the business world, I don't advocate making your boss run through soft sand with a 100-pound log in her arms! But the idea that the boss will admit to and take the hit for a miscue is important. However it's conveyed, Team First should be the guiding principle.

Good Teams Take Possession of Their Leaders

In the course of several weeks of training, you'll see SEAL trainees and teams "take possession" of their leaders again and again. When this happens, we see a lot. We see leaders sharing in team responsibility rather than acting as untouchable, ruthless, reasonless, unaccountable tyrants. It's an important transition.

First, we see the class feeling guilty about someone else being punished for their mistakes. We also see the leaders understanding that accountability doesn't always have to relate to responsibility. As I noted earlier, if you're responsible, you need only find out who or what is at fault. If you're accountable, you take the blame and rectify the situation.

It starts to really sink into everyone's mind how everything you do has an effect on the team. As a leader, your leadership sets the tone for the success of the mission. If officers have the right brand of leadership, we observe an interesting phenomenon, which I believe applies in all leadership situations, not just in the military.

After several weeks of punishing the leaders for the results of the team, the team will voluntarily run to the aid of its officers. They will drop down and do all the physical remediation that the officers are ordered to do even though they aren't required to do it. The instructors yell at the class member to get up and stop doing what they are doing. But the instructors never use the word *recover*. "Recover" is an order to get up and stand at attention. Because SEALs need to understand that an order is not a debate and they cannot hesitate in combat, a strict order isn't used here. We don't want our values to conflict.

Turning Up the Volume for the Team

We rarely yell during BUD/S training. Despite what you see in movies, it isn't really our style. But during these interactions, we do use all types of colorful language to make our point. It's all part of reinforcing the team concept; the yelling is not "me" at "you" but about all of us together. It makes the team stronger.

In some sense, BUD/S training is a matter of self-preservation because the more physical remediation you get, the more likely your body is to wear down, which makes it more likely that you will fail the physical tests. So when the students sacrifice with and for their leaders, it means something because it means that they are less likely to make it through training.

Teamability Starts with the Leader

Teamability means that you suffer for the mistakes of others, and others suffer for your mistakes. If a student doesn't feel some discomfort when someone else, including the leader, makes mistakes, we realize pretty quickly that he might not fit in. We zero in on those students. If they don't have the teamability we are looking for, they won't be around much longer. If team members regularly fail to have empathy or concern about mistakes in the leadership, we also zero in on the officer's leadership to make sure he "gets it." Teamability problems can often start at the top!

> The quality of leadership can ignite
> or destroy a team.

Good Leaders Give Good Team Players Second Chances

We accomplish missions and stay alive by being surrounded by team guys. When I was in charge of BUD/S third phase training, we had a student who failed a swim, which landed him before an Academic Review Board (ARB) that decides whether a student remains in training or is dropped from the program. By the third phase, a candidate is well along through training. This swim was one of the last timed physical evolutions.

The instructor staff was unanimously in favor of giving him another opportunity to meet the required swim time because he had teamability and was the epitome of a team guy. We also knew that his father was a retired senior enlisted SEAL so he had been raised to be a warrior and team player.

I allowed him to rest over the weekend and to take another shot at the two-mile swim; he passed it easily. During this last phase of training, most students are physically broken down and hiding injuries; we take everything into account when making these decisions.

This SEAL was among those who tried to save the squad depicted in *Lone Survivor*. He was killed with my friend Erik Kristensen and 13 other SEALs and crewmen that fateful day. He died a team player.

Sharing the Load

When SEAL Teams undergo an operation, we approach it holistically. The old cliché "You are only as fast as your slowest man" means a lot to us. It means that the helicopter won't leave on a hot extract until the slowest man gets there. We call the guy that comes in last the "banana man," but of course we pick him up anyway. Nobody wants to be the banana man.

For us, no place is more representative of sharing the load than in extreme cold weather environments such as Alaska, Norway, and parts of the Arctic. When you go out for a long-range reconnaissance mission in the cold, it's critical to balance the load so that no one with a particular job specialty carries more weight than any other person.

We accomplish this by developing standard operating procedures (SOPs) for how gear is distributed in order to best accomplish the mission. The radioman may have to carry several heavy lithium batteries; the machine gunner carries hundreds of rounds, at 7 pounds per hundred rounds, in addition to the 23-pound machine gun.

We distribute the load in a manner that ensures usability for the mission and not to overburden a few individuals. We all end up carrying 120 pounds for a long-range reconnaissance so "nobody is getting cheated," as we say. We share the load, even among the "cake eaters," as the enlisted men call the officers.

Good teams share the load and don't allow anyone on the team to suffer more than any other. Of course there are times when certain departments or specialties are burdened more than others, but teams are willing to sacrifice, become swim buddies, and pitch in for the success of the mission and the team.

When your rhythm resonates, it creates momentum; other processes fall in line.

Not Always the Same Old Song:
False Motivation Is Better Than No Motivation

In BUD/S training, we have an expression that helps students deal with adversity: "False motivation is better than no motivation at all." What does that mean? It's a bit counterintuitive, but when you're a team dealing with adversity, it takes only one person to raise the spirits of the team, no matter the circumstances. The ability to pull himself out of his own misery and motivate the team is a very valuable trait in every team guy.

The idea of "false motivation" becomes apparent to the students when they are lying in the surf zone in the 55-degree waters of the Pacific Ocean at two o'clock in the morning, with nothing to look forward to except the sunrise in four and a half hours. As instructors, we let the conditions of cold water and cold air do the work. We stand in front of our four-wheel drive vehicles with the lights on, facing the surf, watching the students do "surf immersion," or what they call "surf torture."

Out of misery, one student will start singing at the top of his lungs. He might just be pissed off, or he may just want the people around him to stop feeling sorry for themselves, take an offensive mindset, and do something about the situation. Once one student starts singing, you can probably imagine what happens next. Before you know it, the whole class is singing in defiance! They forget how miserable they are, and they give each other "false motivation." We've found that motivation is contagious—even if it's false.

(continued)

Here the expression "picking yourself up by the bootstraps" becomes real. When someone on the team defies the misery and moves forward, the wave of motivation can and will follow. Sometimes the students sing songs that the instructor staff doesn't approve of. The instructors yell from the dry beach to stop or else! But the students defy us and keep singing. It's as if to say, "Come in the cold water and *make* us stop, you son of a bitch!"

One person can change everything at the right moment. When you have that, you have First, Fast, Fearless teamability.

It Pays to Be a Winner

Among SEALs, you will hear repeatedly the phrase "it pays to be a winner." In BUD/S training, it tells students that what they do matters. It reminds them that in warfare, the winner goes home at night.

As leaders, it's easy to fall into a common trap: to notice only the bad things, the things that aren't quite perfect. It's another thing to be a winner and guide your team to be a winner. It pays to see the good traits in your team and to recognize what they did right.

In the business world, most of what you do isn't a life-or-death situation. But the winning mentality can bring you much more than if you simply focus on what's wrong or what needs to be fixed. You don't want to just fix something. You want to *win*. If you bring your whole team forward with this attitude, you'll be far more likely to succeed. Remember, two is one and one is none. A whole team marching in unison adds up to a far larger fighting force in the course of First, Fast, Fearless leadership.

TAKEAWAYS

- "Teamability" refers to the ability and willingness to be part of a team, put the team first, sacrifice for the team, and make the team better.

- "Working backward" means taking care of the team, the unit, and the swim buddy first. Then and only then can you take care of yourself. Team First is the guiding principle.

- If we focus on ourselves rather than on the team or the team assets, we won't be ready. For SEALs, it's a matter of life or death, but it applies in other organizations too.

- A swim buddy is the smallest unit of the largest whole, the team.

- All successes, failures, and mistakes are shared across the team, including the leaders.

- When a team "takes possession" of a leader, it strengthens the notion of shared responsibility.

- Team players get second chances.

- When team members sacrifice themselves for the leader, it's both a sign of good teamability and good leadership.

- Teamability starts at the top. It begins with a willingness to sacrifice for the team, to be humble, which is consistent with the First, Fast, Fearless leadership brand.

- Teamability is a key part of a winning mindset.

CHAPTER 13

Developing a Perimeter: An Invisible Shield to Clarify and Protect

SEALs identify strongly with the ancient Spartans and their honor code of brotherhood. The Spartans are celebrated for the Battle of Thermopylae against the Persians in 479 BC. Spartan warriors defended a narrow pass between the mountains of central Greece and the sea, a pass called Thermopylae. They were only 300 strong, with possibly 6,000 soldiers from across Greece in the rear for support. They were the tip of the spear that faced a Persian army thought to number 100,000.

Spartans fight side by side, using their shields to form a powerful perimeter of armor to protect all inside of it. They move and fight as one, not as individuals. Spartan warriors were expected to have the courage to protect their teammates to the end. Courage was so valuable to the Spartans that mothers told their sons as they went off to war, "Come back with your shield, or come back on it." Maintaining the shield was more important than coming back alive.

For two days the small number of Greeks, led by the Spartans, fought off the Persians while inflicting heavy casualties. They held the pass until a Greek traitor went to the Persian king with information about a way, known only to locals, that led to a position behind the Greek army. The 300 Spartans died defending the pass. It took a traitorous deed to defeat the mighty Spartans, who fought side by side until the very end.

In the battle of Ramadi, a battle for control of the Al Anbar province in Iraq, the SEALs became legendary among conventional forces for their aggressiveness and willingness to take the fight to the enemy. This battle during the spring and summer of 2006 proved to be the heaviest combat engagement in SEAL history. It is one of the places the late SEAL sniper Chris Kyle earned the distinction of being the most successful sniper in American history (his story is told in the bestselling book and Academy Award–nominated blockbuster *American Sniper*). It is also where one of our greatest heroes, Michael Monsoor, earned the Medal of Honor, the highest honor that can be given to a member of the Armed Forces. Monsoor sacrificed his own life to save his team. In September 2006, an insurgent threw a grenade onto a rooftop where Monsoor and several other SEALs and Iraqi soldiers were positioned. Monsoor smothered the grenade with his body, saving his comrades from serious injury or death. He died 30 minutes later.

In the SEAL Teams, you often find yourself in environments "owned" by an enemy. That poses a constant and varied threat of danger. You could be out in the field with a 2-man element, a 60-man assault element, or in a base camp surrounded by high cement walls protected by heavily armed soldiers. No matter where you are, one of the fundamental principles of warfare is to constantly maintain a 360-degree security posture, ready to fight any threat. We call that a *perimeter*.

Depending on the terrain and enemy threat, a perimeter is generally shaped like a circle. We form one every time we stop a formation on patrol. When the signal is given to form a perimeter, everyone fans out to their predetermined positions with their swim buddy. From a perimeter the team is postured with forces and firepower distributed equally; it can respond with equal firepower in any direction if contacted by the enemy.

The perimeter defines the team, the enemy, the space, and the action. It is both a physical and virtual boundary. You protect what's inside, and you depend on the teamwork that lies inside. Your "interior lines" allow you to confront the enemy in unison. As all of this implies, one of the worst enemies is the enemy within the perimeter.

Good leaders and managers define the perimeter in everything they do. They support what's inside, allow what's inside to work in unison to protect and to attack, and they guard against any "enemies" within. In so doing, the team effectively looks and acts bigger than it really is.

Great Teams Perform Bigger Than They Are

It has been observed that conventional forces can listen to a firefight happening at a distance and quickly identify the force as being Navy SEALs. When a well-trained and coordinated force gets into a firefight, they can sound several times larger than they actually are. Why? Because they are all firing and fighting in unison, not as individuals. In a firefight, our enemies will often try to break contact, out of fear that they are fighting a force much larger than we actually are.

Although not as loud, similar effects might be observed with teams in the business or enterprise world. A team that works in unison seems stronger and more effective—maybe even more so than it actually is. If you define a perimeter, strengthen what's inside, and make sure it acts, communicates, and moves forward as a team, it will have greater credibility and impact than a loosely guided and coordinated band of individuals. A good leader defines the perimeter and leads all that's inside of it. What's inside the perimeter and how it works together becomes part of the team brand.

> A team *moving forward together* has more credibility than a band of individuals.

Danger: The Enemy Within Is Worse

Particularly in combat, we often observe that the enemy inside the perimeter is worse than the one outside. Infighting and conflict within the team can inflict more damage on a team than the enemy outside the perimeter. It is a leader's responsibility to resolve the pressures team members face and to maintain the resilience of the team during periods of high stress. Teams can endure great amounts of outside stress *if* they keep the enemy outside and their teammates close, and if they are led by competent leaders.

Welcoming Guests and Home Invaders

The inside of the perimeter represents the team and what you want to accomplish through, by, and with them. The enemy and danger should remain outside. The core of the perimeter is composed of our actions to accomplish our mission, our ethos, and the elements of TRUST. Within the perimeter lie mutual respect, fairness, recognition, meaningful work, loyalty, caring, friendship, flexibility, honesty, humility, working together, and all the other positive actions and virtues of a brotherhood.

There are many pressures on a perimeter of a team. They can be especially destructive during times of high stress and fear. In a world of VUCA, there is always pressure on the perimeter. It's easy for people to feel isolated when a team is living in VUCA. The change and uncertainty of VUCA can make people feel powerless, which can lead to helplessness and hopelessness. Over time, I have found that bureaucracies are notorious for having this effect! Bureaucracies can put people on the defensive and in reaction mode—and out of the offensive first strike mindset. Bureaucracies can be considered an enemy within.

The rule of thumb: it's a welcome guest if it's inside the perimeter, and it's a home invader if it's on the outside. What's dangerous to a team should be kept outside the perimeter. Some things you can't control—volatile markets, competitors, and world events. But a strong team with a strong perimeter can deal with those dangers.

Dealing with the Enemy Within

Aside from bureaucracy, there are many enemies that can creep inside your perimeter. As a leader, you should recognize and deal with them. Examples include self-service, contempt, favoritism, unfairness, smugness, complaining, insulting, stonewalling, lying, cheating, and stealing. These ills will destroy a team from within, and they can be, along with the infighting they produce, more destructive than the enemy outside.

Another rule of thumb: anything that doesn't help the team should stay outside. Contempt among teammates is one of the worst. It's such a toxic emotion that in the military it is against Articles 88 and 89 of the Uniform Code of Military Justice (UCMJ) to display contempt against elected officials and senior officers; you can be court-martialed for it! I recommend that you take a similar stance against team members with contempt for each other.

> Your worst enemies may lie inside your perimeter. They are often more destructive.

The Good Kind of Peer Pressure

We all know what peer pressure does to a group. Mostly, we tend to think of *bad* peer pressure, the kind that gets kids into drugs or crime. But the existence of peer pressure in high-performing brotherhoods is a must. As Nietzsche said, "Invisible threads are the strongest ties." In an organization founded on an ethos and a set of values, where people are held accountable for their conduct and the conduct of their teammates, peer pressure—good peer pressure—becomes the strongest police force in the organization. It should be encouraged.

The Power of Shame and Courage

Many people have asked what my biggest fear was going into combat. Most assume it's being killed or severely maimed by an IED, or some other life-changing injury. We all fear those threats, but I believe the biggest fear all SEALs share is letting our teammates down and not having the courage to fight in the face of fear. We fear not stepping up and proving ourselves in combat. At the end of the day, in the SEAL Teams, we fear shame more than anything else. If we were more fearful of death and mutilation, we would not have become SEALs.

Why do we fear shame, and why do we avoid it at all costs? Simply because if you're shamed, the team is placing you outside the perimeter; you are no longer part of the brotherhood. Shame means you don't belong to the team, and we all want to belong.

A team based on virtues in which everyone believes and a team that has the peer pressure to do the right thing is extremely strong. That team has power that only brotherhoods have. Like the Spartans we identify with, we all believe strongly in courage. All heroes display courage. And leaders like Mother Teresa, Martin Luther King Jr., and Mahatma Gandhi—all pacifists—displayed great amounts of courage.

One thing that fascinated and humbled me at the same time was watching the courage of some of the young soldiers I worked with, the soldiers who do most of the actual fighting in our wars. When we go on missions, we coordinate with the conventional Marines and Army soldiers, who are the Quick Reactionary Force (QRF). The QRF is our backup: if we get into trouble and need help, they come to our assistance. When the call is made, these young soldiers don't hesitate; they run to the sound of gunfire.

Why are people who don't really know each other willing to suffer such risk for each other? To me, it's pretty simple. We do it because we know the other guy would do it for us. Courage is the ultimate outcome of good peer pressure. We jump out of airplanes at 30,000 feet, at night, with so much equipment that we can barely stand up. I do it because the guy in front of me did it, and the guys beside me and behind me did it too.

A brotherhood doesn't need a thick volume of rules for people to do the right thing. When people believe in their values, they have the desire to perform. This desire will drive the behavior of the organization. That is why I say, "Never fully trust a teammate who cannot be shamed." If someone breaks way outside the perimeter and does something immoral or against the team and feels no remorse and shame, I don't trust him.

> **If you cannot shame a teammate, you probably can't trust him either.**

Beware the Sound of Beating Drums

At Virginia Military Institute, if students are caught committing an honor code violation, such as lying, cheating, or stealing, they are expelled from the institution. The morning after the cadets are found guilty of an honor violation, the students are

(continued)

185

woken up by the sound of drums. The names of the cadets and their infractions are announced for all to hear as they are expelled. They are shamed out of the school, never to return. The process is called "drumming out."

This may sound like a harsh and humiliating punishment, but it sends a strong message that acting outside the value system is unacceptable. If you adhere to the code, you are safe. If you don't, you not only fail as part of the brotherhood but you're also an unwelcome invader. For any organization to live its values, it must be willing to enforce them and hold everyone accountable.

Shame Is a Double-Edged Sword

As human beings, we are hardwired to be tribal and to live around each other. We are occasionally held back by our own egos and self-serving ways, but I believe we all want to be accepted, even if we don't admit it.

As such, leaders should be very careful never to shame people and put them outside of the perimeter unless they deserve it. That said, if it *is* deserved, disciplinary action should be swift and final. I don't think reprimanding people in public or intentionally disrespecting them is ever acceptable unless the offense is severe enough to warrant kicking them out of the organization.

When someone in the SEAL Team does something so far outside the perimeter—lying, cheating, or stealing—that he breaks trust, he goes to a Disciplinary Review Board (DRB). This DRB of senior leaders in the community uses all five pillars to decide the SEAL's fate. If this board determines a SEAL to be untrustworthy, the Commanding Officer (CO) takes away the Trident that he wears on his chest, which he is never allowed to wear on his uniform again. The CO and SEA gather the entire SEAL Team together to explain why they kicked out the offending SEAL. Again, the SEAL being expelled must deserve it, and his infraction must be meaningful in the eyes of others.

Dealing with Toxic Teammates

We've all heard about the power of motivation esprit de corps. Anyone who has ever worked within a team has come across people who are toxic to the group—people who are nasty, narcissistic, arrogant, condescending, or malicious, people who suck the life out of the room and are a constant drain on the group. Put simply, they are not team players. Not only do such individuals drag themselves down, they infect other team members and damage relationships throughout the perimeter. They silently kill esprit de corps.

Toxic individuals are corrosive to the cohesion of relationships and eventually the team itself. They suck energy out of the team and out of the leader. Of course, it's worse if a toxic individual is the leader. In this case, it must be dealt with swiftly to avoid compromising the whole team.

When individuals have to deal with toxic team members, they can become obsessed with the toxic behavior. The same negative movie plays over and over in their heads; they are likely to look for ways to sabotage the toxic team members. They will spend valuable time and attention on this, which is counterproductive to any mission.

It can pay to have some patience with subpar performance on a team; many trainees can succeed with the swim if you give them another chance and the aid of a swim buddy. A swim buddy might be deployed as well to give a little feedback or encouragement to eliminate toxic behavior. But persistent toxic behavior will eventually corrode the team—and will corrode the team's confidence in you as a leader if you don't deal with it. Toxic teammates need to be drummed out. Deal with it with sensitivity and indirectly if you think that works best—but deal with it.

> As a leader, you must deal with toxic behavior.
> Not dealing with it erodes team confidence in you.

Dealing with Toxic Bosses

Shortly before I retired from the SEAL Teams, I was hiring for a General Schedule (GS) government worker position to run our training ranges across the country. One applicant, whom I'll call Lee, stood out. He was currently working at a higher-level position on the Admiral's staff. It seemed a bit odd that he would want to take a demotion to come work with me, but he did.

I had heard through the rumor mill that this particular applicant was a problem. Although he had more than enough skills, I was warned that he had a tough time getting along with people. I was open with him when I interviewed him for the job. He was respectful and very honest with me as well.

He was a retired Marine officer on the tail end of his second career of government service. He didn't badmouth his boss, but he made it clear to me that he was toxic and that if he didn't transfer, he would resign. Although it would cost him a lot of money in retirement, he was prepared to do it because he couldn't tolerate his boss any longer. I did a little research of my own and discovered that, indeed, everyone who had worked for the boss felt that he was toxic.

I hired Lee. Over the course of the next year, he was a different person. I couldn't have asked for a better team player or someone who was more dedicated to the mission and to the team. It didn't matter how stressful the job became, he was a great performer and understood and respected the power of the brotherhood. He often told me that he didn't care what job he did as long as he did it with good people. I believe we all know the feeling.

The next year, the government faced a sequestration. Word came down that some "nonessential" government personnel would be given leave without pay because of insufficient funding. I'm sensitive, of course, to the fact that "nonessential personnel" are generally paid much less and need the money much more, often living from paycheck to paycheck.

Lee came to me and volunteered to be placed on leave without pay so that others could keep their jobs. He didn't want the lower-paid employees to suffer catastrophic financial hardship. Not only did he request to be placed on leave without pay but he also insisted on continuing to work. He understood what it meant to be a team player.

This is the same behavior from a man who, less than a year earlier, was so full of anger and frustration toward his boss that he was willing to resign rather than continue to work with a toxic leader. Toxic leaders can do more damage than most people think.

The best thing to do with toxic leaders is to get outside their perimeter, to step aside gracefully, if you can. They will eventually corrode the performance of the entire team, you included. You can't drum them out, but you can leave the parade ground.

Protecting the Perimeter: Special Cases

Defining and protecting the perimeter is a vital leadership duty. An effective *steward* leader carries a shield to protect the team by keeping the enemy outside and by strengthening what's inside. Here are a few special cases in which perimeter boundaries and actions aren't so obvious.

Top Performer—but Outside the Perimeter

Every now and then, even top performers must be moved off the team. They perform, but they scorch and burn relationships along the way, and ultimately they make *other* teammates disengaged and ineffective. It is up to the leader to identify these types, too, and to drum them out.

I'm happy to say that I've only done this on a couple of rare occasions, but I have done it. Once, in Iraq, I found an officer deliberately sabotaging the team by sending out misinformation to headquarters in order to shine the light on himself and his unit. I confronted him about it; he smugly admitted his actions. In just over an hour, his bags were packed, and he boarded a helicopter never to return. Almost immediately, team morale shot through the roof, and others took up the slack. Having the wrong person is always worse than having one less person. This was a key leadership moment for me to prove to the team that I would not tolerate dangers inside the perimeter.

> Having the wrong person is always worse than having one less person.

Academy Genius—but Outside the Perimeter

In BUD/S training, we do regular peer evaluations. We do several in each phase to maintain a 360-view of students going through training. We know what we see, but we're not always sure what they see.

During one Hellweek I was running, the instructor staff came to me and wanted to kick an officer out of training, despite the fact that he had completed the week-long event. They had consistently observed this particular officer's poor performance and had documented it on numerous occasions in the logbook.

The officer in question was extremely smart and was in the top of his class at the Naval Academy. He was also a gifted athlete who had no problems with the BUD/S physical standards. But the instructors noticed that his boat crew was always last and they were always fighting among themselves.

The instructors picked up the tracks left by this officer. They noted consistently that he seemed to lead from the rear, not from the front.

We held a Disciplinary Review Board to determine this officer's fate. The board consisted of several instructors and senior enlisted from each phase of training, all of whom I oversaw as the Officer in Charge. As soon as the officer in question walked in, I could see, hear, and feel his arrogance and contempt—and not a shred of humility. I could see it from his posture and bearing, which of course is part of the evaluation. He felt the instructors were treating him unfairly and that he was one of the best leaders in his class.

When he finished speaking, the first thing I asked was, "Who's in your boat crew?" As he named them, I pulled their peer evaluations out of a stack and read them off to him. One by one, the peer evaluations slammed him for being a lazy, toxic, self-serving person who spoke down to people and cared only about himself. Some of them used very colorful language; they had so much to say that they had written on the back of the one-sided form! One remark that I still remember: "If he makes it into the SEAL Teams, I don't want to be a SEAL." That is a powerful statement coming from someone who is willing to give his life for his profession.

As I read through these forms, the arrogance left him. He no longer felt he was being cheated or treated unfairly. He understood clearly that we were on to him and that we wouldn't tolerate a toxic teammate, especially a leader. He was dropped from training that same day. We immediately told the class what we did and why, and they celebrated.

Don't put a Band-Aid on gangrene. If it's outside the perimeter, strengthen within; if it's within, get rid of it, or do your best to minimize its impact. In business, act as a team and strengthen team bonds. Carry the shield, and keep everyone behind it. It's a key part of First, Fast, Fearless leadership.

> Don't put a Band-Aid on gangrene.

TAKEAWAYS

- The perimeter defines the team, the enemy, the space, and the action. It is both a physical and virtual boundary. You protect and depend on what lies inside.

- As a leader, you not only guard against what lies outside the perimeter but you also deal with enemies *inside*—such as bureaucracy and self-serving behavior.

- By defining and maintaining a strong perimeter, you make the team look—and perform—bigger than it really is.

- Shame is a powerful force, and it can be used to keep team members inside the perimeter. If shame doesn't work on someone, you probably can't trust him or her in the first place.

- Strong credentials—even strong performance—don't necessarily put someone inside the perimeter. It takes trust and teamwork above all else.

- Teams can endure a great amount of stress *if* they keep the enemy outside.

- If it's outside the perimeter, strengthen within; if it's within, do your best to get rid of it, especially if it's toxic. Not taking action will erode team trust.

CHAPTER 14

Leading from All Parts of the Line: The Importance of Followership

As the SEAL charter has evolved, we have taken on many core missions to conduct Foreign Internal Defense (FID) operations. However, before 2005, we didn't specifically train to it. Being required to go anywhere, anytime, and do anything beyond our core specialties is quite a responsibility. With limited time and resources, we have to make choices. When the Iraq War began, I didn't know a single SEAL who spoke Arabic, and we had never trained in conducting combat FID operations with a foreign conventional military.

FID is the art of training and fighting with a foreign force to be a force multiplier in wars, as we did in Iraq and Afghanistan. We designate a small American unit to lead a large foreign army. We develop the foreign force, so that when we leave, they can function alone to defend their established government. Prior to the 9/11 attacks, SEALs knew little about conducting FID in a combat zone. But SEALs have an offensive mindset; we are innovators who learn quickly. We knew that our Army Green Beret brethren "do this for a living," so we knew where to go to learn.

In 2005, I found myself in charge of FID missions involving as many as 1,500 Iraqi soldiers. When we first started conducting FID missions with the Iraqis, we had to fall back on our previous training. "You fight like you train," so that's what we did. We set up their training just as we had been trained, minus the physical remediation and performance standards. We couldn't be selective; we had to play the hand we were dealt.

We used the training theory "show, tell, and do," in which we do everything they are supposed to do as a way to teach them how to do it. If it was live-fire assault training, we would perform a room entry, shooting at targets inside the building, and then we would talk them through what we had done and why. Then they would do it, and we would watch and debrief them. As they progressed, we would make the scenarios more difficult and challenging. If they got dirty, we got dirty, and so forth. One of our first tasks was to develop a "train the trainer" program for technical equipment, so we could have our trainers spread out among their units.

Here is where we hit a snag. The Iraqi officers insisted that they train separately from the enlisted soldiers instead of with their unit. When the enlisted trainers began teaching their officers, the officers immediately refused and informed me that enlisted men would not be allowed to teach them— they felt it to be beneath them! As in most socially conservative Middle Eastern countries, in Iraq, the officers are at the top, and the enlisted soldiers are at the bottom. As basic conscripts, they are treated as second-class citizens. There is no "middle class" like the Non-Commissioned Officers (NCOs) we have. Our NCOs are enlisted personnel who attain a certain rank because of their leadership ability and time in service, and they are given a significant amount of authority and responsibility.

There are many cultural and technological differences, but I believe this is probably the single biggest deciding factor in why conventional Arab forces lose wars to the West. They have no NCOs, while NCOs are the foundation and backbone of America's military. They "run the troops" on a daily basis. The Navy has NCOs called Chief Petty Officers who are experts in a field. Generally, they have at least 10 years of experience grooming to be a Chief. Chiefs are the ultimate swim buddy; no SEAL Officer would ever want to lead troops without a Chief by his side.

When you watch the news, you always see Admirals and Generals talking about warfare and strategy, but you never hear from those who actually lead the people who fight the wars, our NCOs. In the Navy, it is our Chiefs. Technically speaking, every enlisted military person is subordinate to every officer, but that doesn't go far enough to explain the relationship.

What *is* the relationship? And what's the greater message here? Simply, that rank doesn't mean everything. Whether or not you outrank someone, you should always act as a leader. And as a leader, you still follow—you follow those in the know and those with the right experience—in spite of your rank or title. Good leaders know how to follow others when the situation calls for it.

It's called *followership*. It is an element of leadership just as important as leading from the top.

Followership: Leading from the Back of the Line

Everyone talks about leadership, but most of us—especially the good leaders among us—are also followers. In the SEAL Teams, there is nothing negative about being a follower. Our ethos states clearly that we expect to lead and be led.

In truth, following with an offensive mindset is leading from a different direction; by no means does it connote being passive or

195

submissive. Our Chiefs in the SEAL Teams provide a great example of how to actively follow someone and how to make following a critical part of leading.

We recruit and train some of the toughest human beings on earth. All consider themselves alpha males. By nature, they aren't passive bystanders. Without a strong sense of followership, it would be impossible for such a group of alpha males to get anything done. Why? Because as we all know, these folks want to be dominant and in charge. I see such behavior in many teams outside the SEAL world, especially executive teams. SEAL leaders and SEAL Chiefs don't see their followership role as submissive or passive; we pursue it aggressively when the time is right.

Watching Chiefs lead and follow for 20 years has taught me the nature of "aggressive following" and the importance of being the right type of leader. If you are a self-serving, ego-based leader, you will turn away the followers you need. Following and leading both require the right brand to get results. If the leader doesn't lead with humility and respect, it will be much harder for the follower to follow in harmony. The advice we give, especially to junior officers, is to focus on the mission, focus on the men—and listen to your Chief.

> **Your brand as follower—not just leader—
> is also important.**

Let Your People Be the Winners

When you're in charge, it's easy to fall in love with your own ideas and to stop taking serious input from the team. Early on, I was told to let your people be the winners—not you. This means that when you are dealing with problems, planning, and decision making, allow your Chief and the team to find the solution and go with their plan when it makes sense. Give them guidance, but let them decide and be in control as much as possible, so they can have ownership. That said, always remember that you are still accountable.

You Fight for a Democracy, but You Don't Work for One

Sometimes my Chief and I would have heated discussions about issues we faced or missions we were on. I expected him to challenge me and to express himself fully; he always lived up to that expectation. In the SEAL Teams, Chiefs have more freedom to speak their minds and be very blunt with the truth because that's what is expected; it's the environment we create.

When these discussions occurred "behind closed doors," we always made a decision before the door opened. We tried to avoid having such discussions in public. When the door opened, the Chief and everyone in that room understood that "you fight for a democracy, but you don't work for one." At the end of the day, accountability rules, and leaders will make decisions not everyone will like. If his ideas were not implemented, a Chief never lets his subordinates know that; he owns the decision and moves forward. The Chief knows that complaining to his subordinates about the decision is unacceptable and severely degrades the chain of command.

> A follower owns the decision too.

It's About Success, Not About Being Right

A follower understands that no plan will ever be successful unless everyone is on board and committed. It's about success, not about being right. Being able to humble yourself as a follower and commit to someone else's decision is critical for any mission success.

A Chief will defend the officer's decision to the end because he trusts him as a leader to do the best for the mission and the team. Being the right kind of leader is critical to getting committed and engaged followers. A self-serving, ego-based leader will break this bond and will never have—or recover—this kind of loyalty and trust. A leader's brand sets the stage for followers to follow.

Most people perceive, incorrectly, that the military is always about giving orders and that things just get done. In a sense, that's true because every decision becomes an order. But the ideas behind those orders don't always come from the officer or leader in charge.

When possible, leaders should always listen to their people's ideas and reserve giving direct orders for when they have to. When leaders let their people decide, it gives their people a greater sense of control over their jobs and ultimately a better sense of ownership.

What most inexperienced leaders don't realize is that this inclusive approach makes direct orders more effective when they must be given without discussion. People won't question the orders if they trust the leader; they will know that he is protecting the perimeter and doing the best he can for the mission and the team, not himself. We all know hindsight will tell us what the best plan was. That's not important. What's important is that when a decision is made, people accept and execute it.

The strength of any team comes from the ability of its followers to execute plans from decisions made. As a leader, you must remember that you are looking for results, and those results lie in the hands of your followers. If you stay married to your own ideas long enough, the team will stop being creative. They won't come to you with solutions. Instead, they will wait to be told, knowing that their ideas won't matter.

> **There are no bad teams—only bad leaders.**

I have experienced being on a staff where the leader thought only his ideas were valid. We were there only to execute his plans. By acting this way, he completely undermined initiative and innovation—and then complained that his staff was not functioning well or being proactive. He had a reputation for complaining about his staffs and how they never meet his expectations.

Leaders are responsible and accountable for getting the most out of the hand they are dealt. Their job is not to complain about the cards. Bitching and moaning about the staff is unbecoming of a leader and is never acceptable. It will waste your time, and worse, it will bring the enemy inside the perimeter. When people hold themselves personally accountable for their teams, they don't make excuses. They figure it out.

Be careful not to stifle followership. It can be toxic to your teams and toxic to performance.

> "My way or the highway" destroys
> followership—and teamwork eventually.

How to Be a Good Follower

Followership is not about being passive or submissive. It's about mirroring leadership. It's about being a leader in how you respond to *your* leaders, and it's about being a leader among the rest of your team. It's about being First, Fast, Fearless; it's about being a *moralist, jurist, teacher, steward,* and *philosopher.* It's about getting others, including your leader, to want to do and to be able to do something important—all despite the fact that you may not be the titular or ranking leader.

You can tell a lot about your own leadership by how the people in your team conduct themselves around you and the team in general. In the SEAL Teams, we often talk about how, throughout their careers, good followers lead like their "sea daddy" led them. They mimic the leadership style they "grew up" under. Each SEAL Team has its own unique subculture because SEALs tend to return as senior leaders to the same SEAL Team in which they came up.

As an example, General Stanley McChrystal, who was in charge of the U.S. forces in Afghanistan and the International Security Assistance Force (ISAF), was a popular leader with a large following of Special Operations personnel. People would keep track of where he was and find their way to his command. These "McChrystalites" conducted themselves as leaders and followers very much the way he did. They were no nonsense, straight to the point, and they made things happen.

Chains of Command, Chains of Abuse

If you are an abusive leader, you establish a climate of abuse. You know what you'll get from your people and how they will treat their people. If you have an abusive leader, as a follower, you have a responsibility to deal with that situation, too, especially if you have subordinates reporting to you.

Abused kids often grow up to become abusive, too, unless they break the chain of abuse. If you feel you are being led badly, as a follower, it is your duty to stop the chain of abuse and shield your people from the top. That means doing everything you can to keep your boss from reaching down into your team and being himself to them. That leader should deal with *you*. Your team will know you have their backs, and they will have yours.

The chain of command works when leaders lead correctly within it. It was very rare for me to ever reach down into the team and reprimand an enlisted SEAL. I would raise the issue with the Chief, and he would sort it out. The only exception was an ethos violation. When that happened, the reprimand was swift, and the Chief joined me.

> Following is just leading from a
> different direction.

The Rhythm of a Good Follower

One of my best followership examples comes from my time as the newly promoted Task Unit Commander for Ramadi. Prior to deployment, as I was hastily building a team, word was out that I was looking for someone to be my second in command and Operations Officer.

"Dave" was a fellow officer of the same rank, and he held a similar position. He came to me willing to leave his position, to work for me, running all the operations of the Task Unit. For him, it wasn't a great career move. It was tantamount to a demotion in position because he would now be working for me. But he recognized the importance of the upcoming deployment and its strategic impact on the success of the war. At this point in the Iraq and Afghanistan wars, we were all stretched thin and had to make last-minute adjustments constantly.

Dave was one of the smartest people I've ever met, and much smarter than I was. He could process massive amounts of information quickly, and he had a photographic memory. I believe he had a perfect score on his SATs. He attended the Naval Academy, a first for a family of Harvard graduates. When I met with him, I knew that he would be a good fit. He was talented and seemed to be "on fire" with whatever he was doing. I also knew that because he had sought me out, he had the humility to follow me, and he had the persona to lead from a different direction.

We immediately created a good interpersonal rhythm for getting things done; he had his strengths and I had mine. From the beginning, I explained my leadership philosophy and what I expected of myself as well as what I expected of him and the team. We were both on the same sheet of music. From this conversation on, we were *stewards* of the perimeter, and we built a team from scratch—while fighting the war.

When You Come with a Problem, Bring a Solution— and Be Prepared

When Dave came to me with a problem, he always had a solution for me to consider. During daily briefings, he was prepared. As any good leader would do, when he briefed me on operations and intelligence, he was a step or two ahead of my questions; he had done his homework. He put time and attention into his work— and that built trust.

Good Followers Give Feedback—Good or Bad

For the nine months that Dave and I served together, I don't recall ever having an argument. We were deep in VUCA. Mortar rounds were exploding inside the camp perimeter daily. The mission changed constantly, resources were constrained, the team was new, the workdays were 20 hours long, and missions were conducted around the clock—stress levels were high. But through it all, we didn't let our egos get the best of us. We were successful because we kept the enemy outside the perimeter.

A few months into the deployment, and once we had our rhythm, we took an operational pause. We stopped all missions for a day and took the whole day off. Somehow our acquisitions specialist was able to acquire some rib eye steaks for the occasion! I've discussed important leadership moments; there are important followership moments as well. I was in my plywood office when Dave came in and sat down.

He had just woken from his longest sleep in months. His hair was sticking up; he was still trying to focus his eyes and get his bearings on the day. There was some normal small talk, but I could tell that this wasn't an accidental visit. He had something on his mind.

He proceeded to discuss the deployment and all the chaos we had endured. He laughed and joked about the weird situations that we had found ourselves in and all the other trials and tribulations of war. Then he looked at me, and out of the blue, thanked me for my leadership during those times. He went on with specific examples and shared that people had mentioned to him how, even in the midst of the chaos and the fear, I maintained my composure and held the team together. They all felt that I had their backs and was looking out for them.

It's hard to express the significance of this message, and of him saying it. By that point, I was mentally and emotionally exhausted, and I very much needed to hear it. Dave knew this. He was not only playing a role; he was acting as a leader. He patted me on the back because I needed it. That day, two Chiefs, one SEAL, and one support Chief came to me and expressed the same thoughts, speaking for the troops.

Such followership strengthens a team beyond what you can imagine. These leadership moments truly bond leaders and followers into a brotherhood. These moments carry momentum into the future; even today, I can feel the strength and the emotions of that day. It eliminated the mental and emotional exhaustion I had at that moment, but more important, it conveyed evidence of a strong and successful team.

I never was sure if they had conspired to come see me or if the meetings were purely coincidental. Either way, it worked. Following is not passive, nor is it demeaning. It's just leading from a different direction. Great leaders inspire their followers to have high expectations of themselves and to have high expectations of their leaders. It's the two-way street to First, Fast, Fearless leadership.

> Good leadership + good followership =
> trust + brotherhood

- Followership is "leading from the back of the line."

- Rank doesn't mean everything. Good followers lead or follow depending on what the situation calls for.

- Followers do all the things and play all the roles that good leaders do, including *moralist, jurist, teacher, steward,* and *philosopher.*

- Followers may lead just as much as leaders do.

- Followers are about being successful, not just about being right.

- Followers own the decision too.

- Good leadership usually brings good followership. Bad leadership will almost always destroy followership.

- Good followers:

  - Listen and are listened to

  - Commit to the decisions of their leaders

  - Keep leaders informed of good and bad news

  - Are prepared

  - Bring solutions, not just problems

  - Have a good "rhythm" with the leader

  - Aren't afraid to take on an abusive leader in the interest of the team

- Followership, just as much as leadership, makes strong and successful teams.

PART III

BATTLE RHYTHM

Turning Brand and Brotherhood into Music

And those who were seen dancing were thought to be insane by those who could not hear the music.

—FRIEDRICH NIETZSCHE

Every culture has its own music. We SEALs refer to ours as our "Battle Rhythm."

Battle Rhythm is an organizational condition, or context, that helps individuals confront the change and VUCA of high-stress organizations—and enables the highest levels of success.

In practice, the rhythm and style of an organization living in VUCA works more like a jazz band jam session than an orchestra. In an orchestra, the conductor directs the rhythm. In organizational terms, it's more like a bureaucracy in which one or a few people in charge hold information and decision-making power.

Jazz, on the other hand, appears less in control. The leader of the band is often hard to spot. Musicians may move at different paces, but they are all on the same sheet of music. Louis Armstrong once said, "Never play anything the same way twice."

Certain patterns and elements create a rhythm to lead SEAL Teams through VUCA and situations of dramatic change and adversity. These patterns operate almost subconsciously and tend to lead to better decision making, problem solving, innovation, and results by pushing authority down the organization through a high degree of trust.

No two teams will have exactly the same Battle Rhythm, but just as with jazz, consistent and recognizable patterns set the right conditions for success.

CHAPTER 15

No Man Left Behind

Since the inception of the SEAL Teams in 1962, SEALs have been engaged in every American conflict. We've been involved in overt operations in Iraq and Afghanistan and covert operations that remain highly classified to this day. During all of these missions and often under extreme combat conditions, we have never left a man behind on the battlefield. It is known throughout the organization that if you go into harm's way, we will come get you, no matter what it takes.

The most famous example was depicted in *Lone Survivor*, in which four SEALs were overrun by a large group of enemy Taliban in the remote mountains of the Hindu Kush in Afghanistan. Three of the four SEALs were killed in the firefight, leaving only Marcus Luttrell as the lone survivor. He had no communications with friendly forces, was severely wounded, and was evading a pursuing enemy. The only time the rest of his Task Unit even knew they were in trouble was when Lieutenant Mike Murphy exposed himself to lethal enemy fire to make a satellite call back to the team to report a Troops in Contact (TIC).

Lieutenant Murphy's willingness to expose his position to the enemy so that he could contact headquarters cost him his life and eventually earned him the Congressional Medal of Honor, our nation's highest award. I am proud to have had the honor of training Mike during his final phase of BUD/S training. We knew he was a team player and a great leader. That day, he proved it with the ultimate sacrifice. Today he is a hero among heroes.

When his call made it to HQ, the SEAL Team loaded helicopters and went in for support. The lead helicopter was shot down during the insert, and all of the SEALs and the crew members on board were killed. After the helicopter was shot down, every military force and asset in the area became focused on getting to the SEALs to make sure that no man was left behind.

Navy SEALs don't have a patent on this philosophy. Every military unit lives by this code of willingness to venture into harm's way to save teammates. In exploring the "no man left behind" metaphor for the business world, what I'm really getting at is simple: when teammates feel that their organization truly has their backs and will take care of and protect them, a strong bond of loyalty is created. They don't feel isolated. They are not just a "number." They feel important and valuable. It sends a clear signal throughout the organization that teammates are safe inside the perimeter and will be backed by the team.

When I give talks, people ask, "What does this look like in the real world?" (I love it when people refer to "the real world" as if my world wasn't real, but I know what they mean.) It may work in the military, but how does it apply to civilian life? If you are in an organization and you want people to be engaged and loyal, you must do the same and not leave them behind.

No Man Left Behind—in "One Minute"

My "real-world" example is from a leader, a fellow author, and good friend Ken Blanchard. If you're reading this, there's a good chance you're familiar with his many books on leadership, *The One-Minute Manager* being the most famous among them.

Blanchard is one of the bestselling authors on the subject of leadership—and for good reason. His company, the Ken Blanchard Company, teaches leadership to corporations around the world. Ken bases his leadership philosophy on caring about people. His company thrives because his philosophy works.

I first met Ken in 2001, while attending the University of San Diego to earn my master's degree in executive leadership. (Ken and his wife, Margie, sponsor the degree program.) It was a life-changing experience.

I started the program a few months before the 9/11 attacks. When they happened, I almost dropped out to deploy. At that time, we didn't know it would be a marathon war, not a sprint. We didn't know then that we would all see action. I was fortunate to finish the program and test what I had learned in it on the ultimate stressful playing field: the battlefield.

Everyone Makes It to the Finish Line

During the Great Recession of 2008 to 2010, every business felt the impact of the declining economy, including Ken's. When times are tough, organizations cut the "nice-to-haves" and "trim the fat" all around. His company saw a 25 percent drop in revenues, which is significant in any business.

But Ken, true to "eating his own cooking," recognized that leadership was not a nice-to-have and set out to make the right decision as a leader about what to do about the downturn. Ken got his executive team together. One option on the table was to cut back, as many organizations do—that is, to identify certain positions as nonessential and eliminate them to cut costs.

But, for Ken, that would be the last option.

During the master's program, Ken often repeated his philosophy: "Everyone makes it to the finish line." It's the same among SEALs. No man is left behind. When times get tough, we don't abandon each other. Teams stick together and pull each other along. Ken sent a message throughout the company challenging everyone to find a solution to trim the fat, but he insisted the plan leave no one behind. Laying off people as a way of cutting costs was not part of the plan.

Instead of trying to solve the problem from the top down, Ken tasked his people—*all* of his people—to find a solution. He didn't just rely on the senior executives. He knew that people in their respective departments knew more about how to trim the fat than anyone at the top could know. "The higher you go, the less you know, but the more you owe." However, after the first round of cuts, the numbers still didn't work. The economy was really tough, companies were pulling back severely on training, and Ken's company continued to experience a drop in revenue. Ken asked his folks to come back with another round of cuts.

The plan that came back this second time called for everyone to take a pay cut, including Ken and the other owners of the company. This was the plan Ken adopted because he saw it as a leadership moment, an opportunity to show his people that he was willing to walk his talk and do everything he could to leave no one behind. Ken knew how important it was for a dedicated servant leader to take care of his people. Be loyal to them, and they will take care of you and watch your back. You don't get one without the other.

> **Walk the talk, and never leave anyone behind.**

"Invisible Threads Are the Strongest Ties"

Imagine how powerful Ken's signal was throughout the company. Although difficult to measure, people appreciated it and became more loyal to the mission than ever. Ken didn't treat them like numbers on a spreadsheet but like the human beings they are. He didn't manage. He led.

According to Nietzsche, "Invisible threads are the strongest ties." I am a strong believer in this concept. There is nothing stronger than this type of loyalty to your people; they don't forget it. Our Texas SEALs like to say, "You will have to pull back on the reins, but you won't have to give them the spurs." True brotherhoods have initiative because they do not want to let each other down. Over the years, I've had a lot of contact with the Blanchard team members. Never have I heard anyone complain or badmouth the company. They all wear their Blanchard badges with pride—and love working there.

> **Don't manage. Lead.**
> **Especially** when times are tough.

Left, but Not Left Behind

In the early 2000s, I was living in England and attached to the British Special Forces. I realized that the SEALs and the British organization had a lot in common. But we also did things very differently in some respects. The unit of the British Special Forces that I was working for had the badge motto "By strength or guile." If they couldn't destroy their enemies with force, they would use clever—some would say "sneaky"—tactics to defeat them.

This unit was a master of subtlety. Beyond their combat operations, however, they had gone one step further than the SEALs to avoid leaving their men behind. They had a department within their organization that was set up exclusively to help their people transition to civilian life after their service. No matter how long their people had been in service, whether for 4 years or for 30, they made a point to take care of them even as they were leaving.

Needless to say, a profession in Special Operations is very stressful and requires a great deal of sacrifice from a person and his or her family. The British understood this and respected it no matter the length of service performed. When the moment came to leave the service, it was time to go and speak to "Wally." Wally had an office inside the camp, and he was there to help each person explore his or her talents and to find another profession. He was very well connected, and he had countless opportunities available to people leaving the British Special Forces.

Are SEALs Left Behind When They Leave?

I spent most of my adult life in the SEAL Teams, and I'm thankful for the opportunity to have served in the capacity that I have. I love the SEAL Teams and my brothers.

Some years after my deployment with the Brits, when I was Training Officer for basic and advanced SEAL training, I tried to implement such a transition program, but I didn't get the response I had hoped for. The Commanding Officer and the senior enlisted SEALs thought such a program would encourage SEALs to leave—it would hurt retention—so it was shot down.

I believe that no former SEAL should be left behind. One thing we don't quite get right is taking care of people when they decide to move on. The SEALs is such a mission-driven organization that if you're getting out and you are no longer part of the mission, no resources are spent to help you transition. Holding true to the spirit of constantly training and looking for ways to improve, I believe the SEAL organization has some work to do on how we treat SEALs as they decide to move on. I hope this is corrected sooner rather than later.

In November 2014, SEAL Team member Robert O'Neil came out publicly and stated that he had shot Osama bin Laden. I cannot speak of any classified information, so I can neither confirm nor deny anything he has said about the mission. But I will use him and his situation as an example of this SEAL Team weakness of not taking care of people as they leave.

Rob is a highly decorated Navy SEAL, one of the most decorated SEALs in our history. After almost 17 years, he left the service, short of the normal 20-year retirement. If he had stayed just 3 more years, he would have received a lifetime pension and many other benefits. So what happened? I don't know all the details, but my question is to his leadership: How did they allow him to leave empty-handed? Rob had been in combat for so long, he needed to get out. This is not uncommon in the SEAL Teams. But as I see it—and consistent with our ethos—we shouldn't allow people to make hasty decisions when they are exhausted from war. Instead, we should take care of them and give them a chance to decompress.

I offer this story as an isolated critique of the SEALs and also as an important lesson for true team leaders in organizations. Your responsibility to look after your people's interests shouldn't expire when they leave your team. If you're loyal to them, they will be loyal to you, even after they depart. They will help you however they can from wherever they are. Most important, it serves as a good example to the team members who remain.

Out the Door, Still Part of a Brotherhood

The Brits knew that how they treated their people when they had endured enough said a lot about the organization. They knew it sent a subtle message that even though they were moving on, the team still cared about them. As such, those who remained knew that when it was their turn to leave, they'd be taken care of as well.

The idea for a similar transition program was rejected because the SEAL leadership believed it would encourage SEALs to leave the organization. While I agreed that it might decrease retention in the short run, I am convinced, based on the British experience, that it would make the team stronger in the long run.

How you treat someone on the way out the door will be observed and internalized by the people who remain. A disgruntled employee will always be more willing to bash the company than a happy one is likely to praise it. It's about reputation, and it doesn't require a ton of resources to do the right thing.

> **Take care of them even after they leave.**
> **The rest of the team will take note.**

No Man Left Behind: It's All About Love

During the troubled times of the Great Recession, Ken Blanchard proved to his people that he would do everything he could to protect them. He did not resort to laying off people, and *everybody in his company knew that was his intent.* He and the other owners personally sacrificed profits so that team members would be protected from losing their jobs.

Many people think that the opposite of fear is courage. As far as I'm concerned, they aren't opposites. Courage is accomplishing something despite your fears. As I've said earlier, the opposite of fear is *love.*

Many fears—of failure, being shamed, being inadequate—get in the way of teammates becoming a brotherhood. Once a brotherhood is bound together by the power of love, the brotherhood eliminates fear. Love and brotherhood keep you going when the chips are down, and the notion of "no man left behind" is a big part of this brotherly love.

> If you leave them behind, they will leave *you* behind. It's a little like love.

Remember, invisible threads are the strongest. Love is one of the strongest of these invisible threads. Love is the difference between being on a team and being in a brotherhood. Love is what makes people run toward the sound of gunfire for each other. It's love that will leave no man behind.

What you face in corporate life may not include the sounds of gunfire, but the same principles apply. If you treat your people as a brotherhood, care about their needs and interests at all times, help them when the chips are down, and leave no one behind, even after they're gone, that brotherhood will accomplish great things. It's all part of First, Fast, Fearless leadership.

TAKEAWAYS

- If you want people to be loyal and engaged, be loyal to them. Never leave them behind.

- When times are tight, layoffs should be one of the last actions to consider. Don't take the easy way out.

- Leaders lead a team as an all-inclusive unit through all activities and at all times.

- Be loyal to people even *after* they leave. They will be loyal to you, and it will demonstrate your loyalty to the ones who remain.

- "No man left behind" is a critical component of brotherly love, which gets the best teams to perform at the highest levels.

Leading at the Speed of War

*I've always found that the speed of the boss is
the speed of the team.*

—LEE IACOCCA

Prior to 9/11, the military hadn't been in a sustained engagement since Vietnam. The decades-long Cold War gave rise to the military bureaucracy. Decision making went from the "boots on the ground" to the top of the chain of command. With nuclear consequences, all decisions were so strategic that they had to be pushed up. But the wars we found ourselves in after 9/11 could not be fought in this typical bureaucratic military system.

War is fast and often lethal and permanent. It requires quick decision making and the ability to deal with all the uncertainties and fears of combat. As we say in the SEAL Teams, the enemy has a vote, meaning if we sit around on the defensive long enough, the enemy will decide for us by attacking and changing the landscape of the battlefield.

Many civilians I talk to about the speed of war think about how long the wars in Iraq and Afghanistan have been going on. But during war, the one thing you can count on is change. The enemy is always voting.

The world of business today has many of the same environmental stresses as war. In the technology industry, if you do nothing long enough, what you were planning to do becomes obsolete. And your competitors are always voting and changing the landscape of the marketplace.

You must always lead. You must always lead at the speed of war.

I can't tell you how many missions we were planning to go on when, suddenly, the enemy voted and decided to move out. All the deliberate planning done earlier was no longer valid. If we wanted to confront the enemy, we had to adjust and make new plans quickly. On such short notice—and when the enemy has a vote—a bureaucratic approval process would be catastrophic.

Leading at the speed of war means making the *right* decisions at the *right time*. I don't mean the *fastest* decisions but ones made at the right time—*timely* decisions that consider what's important but don't impair progress. Leading at the speed of war means making decisions without perfect information. It means avoiding bureaucracy.

Leading at the speed of war requires you to trust your teams, to reap the fruits of the seeds of teamwork and brotherhood that have been sown up to this point. It means joining your troops in war, to know more, learn the truth, gain trust, and react faster. It means allowing yourself to move outside your comfort zone. Otherwise, you'll get bogged down, won't react, or can't decide. It means focusing on what's right, not what's wrong—too much focus on what's wrong will slow you down.

Leading at the speed of war is a system based on well-orchestrated values, teamwork, and timing. When it works, it creates music. It's a key part of the First, Fast, Fearless leadership style.

> **Leading at the speed of war is based on well-orchestrated values, teamwork, and timing. When it works, it creates music.**

A "Leading at the Speed of War" Game

This idea was tested in 2002, during one of the largest war game exercises ever conducted by the military. The exercise was called the Millennium Challenge. This large-scale exercise integrated computer tactics with real forces, and it involved live exercises with over 13,500 troops in 25 different locations across the United States. It was said to have cost as much as $250 million. The intent of MC02, as it was referred to, was to test command and control while transitioning to the world's new technologies, specifically those that enable network-centric warfare.

The exercise involved two teams. The Blue Team was America, while the Red Team represented the enemy, an unknown adversary in the Middle East. Blue had conventional leadership but also a sophisticated electronic surveillance network, imagery, and weapons. Red was a conventional force led by retired Marine Lieutenant General Paul Van Riper, a highly decorated officer who had fought guerilla warfare in Vietnam. Red used human-centered tactics in its fight against Blue. Van Riper knew what it meant to fight on an ever-changing battlefield using conventional and unconventional tactics.

Bureaucracy Happens Because the Enemy Isn't Voting

Blue was led by senior military leaders who had risen through the ranks during the Cold War. They brought the bureaucratic and hierarchical style of leadership that tends to form in the military during times of peace (because the enemy isn't voting). It's not unlike the business world where companies may become complacent in the absence of competition.

When the enemy isn't voting, decision-making authority tends to get pushed higher and higher up the chain of command—so high that people who should be making decisions can't. When this happens, innovation and a quick response disappear, and the organization becomes stagnant. But in the marketplace, the enemy is almost always voting and is seldom sitting still. A big technology "vote" from the market can change an industry overnight.

Companies—like military leaders—that can move at the speed of war can work through these changes. Those that are slow to move, bureaucratic, and defensive will not.

> **In the marketplace, the enemy is almost always voting and seldom sits still.**

In Command and Out of Control

Bureaucracy is a natural result—and cause—of slow-moving organizational behavior. Once enveloped by bureaucracy, even the best leadership has a tough time leading at the speed of war. Good leaders should avoid bureaucracy. Instead, they should focus on customers and competitors and prepare the teams to be ready to move out at any time. If a leader inherits a bureaucracy from others, he or she should do whatever possible to make it smaller or deal with the effects, all while informing everyone on the team why that's important.

There are more specific things a leader can do to speed up decisions and action, which I refer to as "in command and out of control." You can lead by delegating. You can make decisions without perfect information. You can adopt a bias for action to move further and faster, while not being chained by the chain of command.

Napoléon himself said that a General never knows anything with certainty, never sees his enemy clearly, and never knows positively where he is. In MC02, General Van Riper knew that *at best* he could give his troops the support and guidance they needed and *let them* take the appropriate action in the field. He set the framework and *then* delegated responsibility and minor decisions to his team. Here's where trust enters the picture—a values-driven team that has established trust up and down the chain of command can do this.

> **A values-driven team with established trust is fertile ground for delegation.**

Blue, on the other hand, like many bureaucracies, had long staff meetings to present detailed information to the senior leaders. After deliberation and approvals by senior leaders, a decision would be made. The senior leaders always wanted more information before making a decision. They had a "zero defects" mindset. Before the 9/11 attacks, "zero defects" was a term used for the type of environment bred in the military in which one mistake could end your career. Consequently, nobody would take a risk. While Blue operated in this context, Van Riper directed Red to go after Blue with a well-delegated, well-communicated, offensive first strike mindset.

In a short time, "inferior" Red, using asymmetrical warfare (involving surprise attacks by small, simply armed groups) was beating Blue! Red had sunk a major portion of Blue's ships. The results were so lopsided that the exercise was restarted, and the ships that had been sunk were resurrected. Good on-the-ground leadership won the day. Unfortunately, the story doesn't end there.

In the most ironic of twists—illustrating the illusions of bureaucratic command and control—the MC02 exercise was seen by the very bureaucratic players engaged in the exercise as rigged! MC02 was restarted to ensure victory for Blue, the "bureaucracy" team.

When the war game was restarted, its participants were forced to follow a script drafted to ensure a Blue victory. Red was given restrictive parameters to allow Blue to exercise its form of command and control. Among the rules imposed by this script, Red was ordered to turn off their antiaircraft radar, allowing them to be destroyed, and they were not allowed to shoot down any aircraft bringing Blue troops ashore. Van Riper claimed that he wasn't allowed to use his tactics, nor certain weapons or reconnaissance systems. Of course, Blue won!

Van Riper was extremely critical of the scripted nature of the new exercise and resigned in the middle of the war game. He later said that the exercise had been altered to "reinforce existing doctrine and notions of infallibility within the U.S. military rather than serving as a learning experience" and that "the war game was rigged so that it appeared to validate the modern, joint-service war-fighting concepts it was supposed to be testing."

Bottom line: be the leader. Don't let the bureaucracy lead. And don't rely on elaborate tests to measure good leadership.

Leave Your Fortified Compounds

Van Riper knew what our senior leaders would come to learn and live—that is, leaders cannot know everything and cannot be everywhere at all times to make all the decisions. But they do need to be aware and to put themselves in the best position to make the best decisions they can. In Iraq, for a long time after IEDs started taking a heavy toll on American troops, everyone became apprehensive about moving around the cities. By failing to get boots on the ground, we ultimately lost situational awareness.

This happens repeatedly in the business and enterprise world. Managers stay in their ivory towers and are ignorant of what's really going on. In the early days of HP, Bill Hewlett and David Packard stressed *managing by wandering around* (MBWA) to take the pulse of the organization, to know what was going on, and to gain the respect of the troops on the floor.

In Iraq, eventually, our forces took the risk, left the fortified compounds, and started moving about the population to see for themselves what the situation really was on the ground. Great leaders have great staffs that they can trust, but to be available, they must get out and move among the people. It's the best position from which to lead.

The World Smells Like Fresh Paint

A good friend with whom I worked in the British Special Forces received a medal from the Queen of England. My British friend said the Queen had asked him about his children; he informed her that he had a son in school. She then asked him where his son went to school. My friend was surprised and replied, "He goes to school where I live," and he thought to himself, "Where else would he go?" But in royal circles, children go to the finest boarding schools.

He said they have an expression in England: "To the Queen, the world smells like fresh paint." That's because she's protected from the realities of normal, everyday life. Wherever she goes, people scrub the buildings clean, so to her, the world must smell like fresh paint and cleaning solvent.

As a leader, if you insulate yourself from your people, you won't get the truth—that is, the reality "outside the walls." The same goes if you throw up virtual walls by being nasty and unapproachable. You have to move about to get a feel for the environment, the *atmosphere*.

When you lead a trusted brotherhood, you can trust what your staff tells you, but nothing replaces seeing things for yourself. You will get a few more bits of tangible or intangible information and gain more trust with your teams. Some senior leaders don't take to this well because they find out things that they didn't want to know. Facing reality doesn't appeal to some leaders, but remember, insulating yourself from it is the surest road to failure!

As a leader, if you start to smell fresh paint everywhere you go, you're not getting the truth. Worse, your leadership style may have set up those conditions in which people are not telling you the truth.

> **If you start to smell fresh paint everywhere, you're probably not getting the truth.**

Leading by Wandering Around

General McChrystal was big on "getting out of the fortified compound" even as the head General in charge. He would show up in combat gear and go out on missions with the troops—not as a leader but just as a shooter. He would make it very clear to the Officer in Charge, a ground force Commander, that he was taking orders from him and not the other way around. Nothing replaces seeing what is happening on the ground. It also shows the troops that you care enough about them to come see their situation for yourself. You find out if the "boots on the ground" understand the mission. It is also a gesture of empathy and humility.

In the military, one might have to risk life and limb to make this happen. But that's not the case in the business world, so hit the floor!

Go Light and Freeze at Night

In the SEAL Teams we use the expression "go light and freeze at night" to describe how to maneuver and plan operations on the battlefield. When you go out with heavy equipment, it slows you down and makes you less agile; thus, you will be more likely to need more protective equipment! It can be a vicious circle.

When we go on operations lasting for days, we don't bring all the gear that may give us some extra comfort while sleeping in a ditch but that will also slow us down when fighting the enemy. After all, the mission is the focus, not being comfortable. The order of priority for equipment is "bullets, bombs, and comms" (communications). Everything else is nice to have but will slow you down. With this equipment, you can either shoot it, blow it up, or call someone else to destroy it. With an extra blanket, you can do none of the above.

A successful organization moving at the speed of war should process everything they do this way. Every Special Operations Command learns to streamline their organization in order to be able to maneuver quickly. We would limit PowerPoint briefings to black and white, so staff personnel didn't waste their time "prettying up" something that didn't need it. They focused on the mission, not the presentation. Obviously, if the color and pictures were necessary, they were included, but if they weren't, it was a black-and-white deck that led off with the BLUF: bottom line up front.

We structured everything so as to not waste time on things that didn't affect the mission. Our meetings had a simple, consistent structure. Reports and presentations all had the same template, so everyone up and down the chain of command knew how they were going to send and receive information. It's easy for staffs to focus on "feeding the bureaucratic beast" instead of putting their effort into the mission. We have a phrase for that: "self-licking ice cream cones."

Economy of Effort: The 80 Percent Solution

Most things we do in staff positions suffice with what we call the "80 percent solution," meaning the leader just needs the BLUF, the results, and the important information. He doesn't need the bells and whistles and pretty packaging. Economy of effort is the goal, not only for the presenter but also the receiver.

I have seen the "window dressing" required by top "leaders" expand exponentially as you move down the chain of command. This may seem strange, but I have seen Ground Commanders changing the font size on their PowerPoint mission brief minutes before they went out the door to appease the Commander approving the mission. That lost time prevented the unit from doing its rehearsals, a key part of planning. The Commander involved had been groomed during the bureaucracy of the Cold War era.

If you, as a leader, require such formalities and niceties on a presentation, not only will it waste the time of your subordinates but it will also tell me that you're incompetent or insecure about your competency to make the "big" decisions. You're choosing to focus on detail and protocol instead. I've seen it happen countless times in military and nonmilitary settings. Don't fall into this trap.

> **Nix the fancy PowerPoints. At the end of the day, they may only reflect your insecurity.**

It Pays to Be a Winner: Looking for the Positive

In BUD/S training, you hear constantly from the instructors, "It pays to be a winner." Frequently, the students and their teams compete against each other; the winner gets rewarded by taking a break and not having to do the next physical event. It's not about punishing the ones who didn't win the race. It's about rewarding those who did. This is not a negligible difference. It's a very significant shift toward a First, Fast, Fearless mindset.

In organizations it's easy to focus on what people did wrong and to take for granted what they did right. It tends to be easier to find the faults of others than to appraise and appreciate their accomplishments. It's human nature.

As leaders, we must correct mistakes rapidly—particularly ethos mistakes. But it's more important to set a climate where it pays to be a winner. That means that when we see something people do right, like being a team player, sacrificing for others, being fair, or anything else "inside the perimeter," we need to acknowledge it with a pat on the back. We all need it from time to time.

Napoléon once said, "A soldier will fight long and hard for a bit of colored ribbon." We've all seen Generals and Admirals wearing chestsful of medals and ribbons. Those medals are on their chests for a reason: a moment of recognition of what they've done and the glory they have earned in doing so. It's a roadmap, of sorts, of their accomplishments for everyone to see.

Most warriors will swear that we don't care about medals or glory; we are just doing our jobs. That's the party line. But I'll be the first to tell you that we all care about recognition, and when we don't get it, I've seen some people become very upset about it. Medals can be double-edged swords. You give them out to people who do great things, but when you don't give them out to those who think they did great things, it has the reverse effect. It's rare, but it does happen. Although each award has its own criteria, it's still subjective. I'm really talking only about the combat awards displayed in the top rows, not the others typically displayed at the bottom.

> **If you want people to be winners, treat them like winners.**

Not a Medal, but a Letter Home

When I was the Task Unit Commanding Officer in Iraq, I decided to write a letter to the families of all those in my command, describing to them what a great job the men were doing and how they were making an impact on history. I already had the address of everyone's next of kin in case the worst happened and they had to be notified. I decided to send the letter at the halfway point of their deployment because I knew the families worried about the safety of their loved ones. I also knew that none of the families knew me; I wanted to assure them that we were all taking care of each other.

Once the letters made it to their destinations, the men started to receive emails from their families telling them that they'd received it and were proud of them for what they were doing; they cherished the letter. At the time, I had over a hundred Americans working in the Task Unit from different branches of service and from different professions in the military; only about a third were SEALs. In short order, people came to my plywood office with a list of names, asking if I would send a letter to the people on the list. Apparently, these letters resonated; every family member took great joy and pride in the letter. My team members also took pride in the recognition, knowing that their families were sharing the letters with others.

Before I knew it, I had sent out about a thousand of these letters to my troops' families. My SEALs quietly came into my office at zero dark thirty (of course!) with their lists, but they still came. Everyone needs and wants a pat on the back, even a steely-eyed Navy SEAL. When it's personal, it is so much more effective.

I was told that many of the recipients had framed the letter and hung it in their homes, exhibiting their pride in their service member; I'm sad to say the only family that didn't get a letter was mine. It's lonely at the top sometimes!

Appraise and Praise at the Speed of War

I've always been surprised by how well a detailed appraisal is accepted and what a difference it makes in performance. That doesn't just mean a generic pat on the back when teams succeed at something big. "It pays to be a winner" is an atmosphere you create by giving specific appraisals along the way, and not just for the big win. As the letters illustrate, it should be somewhat personal, not always limited to a professional courtesy. If it's inside your perimeter, notice it and reward the behavior. It shows you care about them and that you are paying attention. A meaningful appraisal shows as much humility as an authentic apology.

When you lead at the speed of war, you must appraise quickly, positively, and in a manner consistent with the mission. Being somewhat personal is good; making it totally personal is bad. A First, Fast, Fearless leader always finds the right balance.

> A meaningful appraisal shows as much humility as an authentic apology.

TAKEAWAYS

- Leading at the speed of war means:
    - Making the right decisions at the right time
    - Making decisions without perfect information
    - Avoiding bureaucracy
    - Trusting your teams and brotherhood—and delegating to them
    - Joining the fight with your teams and "managing by wandering around"
    - Allowing yourself to move outside your comfort zone
    - Keeping it positive and to the point
    - Appraising quickly, positively, and consistent with the mission
- The enemy is almost always voting. When they don't vote, the decision-making authority tends to rise higher up the chain of command, leading to bureaucracy.
- Being in command doesn't necessarily mean being "in control" of everything.

- If everything seems perfect and in order ("smells like fresh paint"), it probably isn't—and you probably aren't getting the truth.

- BLUF (bottom line up front) is always best.

- Don't be a fault finder. Make sure you appraise the good in people and the good things they do. Treat them like winners, and they will *be* winners.

CHAPTER 17

Outside the Box: How to Enhance Team Innovation and Problem Solving

The attempt to develop a sense of humor and to see things in a humorous light is some kind of a trick learned while mastering the art of living.

—VIKTOR FRANKL

It was Halloween week, 2001. I was the Officer in Charge of the midnight-to-8-a.m. shift of Hellweek when I first met Charlie. He wasn't like the other students. Charlie was a pumpkin, a fitting new recruit for the time of year. Now, anyone else who might have introduced an actual pumpkin to the BUD/S class could hardly have kept a straight face, but Monty, my SEA could—and did. Monty was a muscular guy, with a shaved head and the looks of a killer, who can talk with extreme authority in any situation without coming out of character. But he can also be a clown, like most of our team guys.

Like the rest of us, he knows our profession is too serious to be taken too seriously. When he introduced Charlie to the class, you could see them struggling to register what he was saying and why he was saying it.

Having just started Hellweek, they were at the highest levels of VUCA. While loud sirens filled the night, we had just spent hours firing automatic weapons into the air and throwing explosives and smoke grenades as we hosed the trainees with freezing water and screamed at them, "Break out!" (that is, "Break out" of your civilian lives). It's total chaos, and it's how we always start Hellweek to get the candidates into the mindset of war. At this point, they are shocked and scared and already physically spent.

The class was instructed to take care of Charlie and to learn everything there was to know about him. We would quiz them during the week to see how much they had "learned" about Charlie. He went everywhere they went; they knew they had better take care of Charlie or we would take care of them! This began on Sunday at dusk; it wasn't until Thursday right before midnight that Monty discovered the awful truth: just a couple of hours earlier Charlie had been crushed in the surf zone while the students were paddling ashore.

Like the great teammates we are, we buried Charlie together, so we decided to do a Viking funeral. We found a wood pallet, and the students built a flammable shrine and put Charlie on it. Two students volunteered to wade out into the bay to light Charlie's pallet on fire and push him out into the tide and to open water. At this point, to volunteer to get in the water is a huge sacrifice; the students have been in and out of the frigid water all week—being almost dry is priceless. With bodies chafed from chest to shins, the saltwater stings everywhere. Without skipping a beat, Monty "invited" the class to join the wake in the water and asked them all to say a little something about Charlie. The students, not wanting to get into the water, responded hilariously, some crying like babies and being held up by their classmates. Only at the end of the funeral, did Monty break character to tell them how silly they looked. But the point had been made: humor and playfulness is one of the best weapons to fight adversity.

From the beginning of SEAL time in the 1940s, our "naked warrior" forefathers were known to have a playful demeanor, despite facing a life of danger and fear. The Naked Warriors, a.k.a. the Underwater Demolition Team (UDT), of World War II swam up to the beaches during major amphibious landings to clear obstacles and mines on the beach, so that the Marines and other soldiers could invade. They swam onto the beach of Agat, Guam, and posted a sign reading, "Welcome, Marines, Agat USO—2 blocks—courtesy UDT4!" Imagine the Marines coming ashore and seeing that smartass sign. What a morale booster it must have been!

Humor and Play: Weapons Against Adversity

It might sound counterintuitive, but a SEAL Team is a pretty playful place to work. For one, a great way for leaders to show humility is to be self-deprecating. SEAL leaders are known for this. In contrast, leaders who lead with their egos are willing to have fun at the expense of others but not themselves—never a good thing.

As a young officer, I learned the power of this sort of humor from one of my leaders; it has served me well in my career. As a leader, I was always very careful to make fun of myself—but not make fun of others, especially not my subordinates—or of the situation because that tends to resonate with people.

If deployed properly, the right amount and the right *kind* of humor can relieve tension and take the team "outside the box," even for just a few short moments of relief. That can have immense value for your teams, not only releasing pressure but also inducing them to think creatively, which paves the way to innovation.

> Our profession, like most professions, is too serious to take too seriously.

Work Hard, Play Hard

We have all heard the expression "work hard, play hard," but in reality, SEALs don't separate the two: Why not play at work? In fact, a big reason to do so is to manage fear.

Studies indicate that fear hinders the abilities of the frontal lobe of your brain, often referred to as the *brain's executive system*. This area is responsible for, among other things, abstract reasoning, paying attention, problem solving, planning, ethical behavior, and mental flexibility. It is also where innovation and creativity take place. Fear inhibits this executive system, and it lowers productivity in every respect. As SEALs, we must control and deal with fear to ensure our continued ability to innovate and problem solve as if our lives were at stake—because they often are.

Many companies have started to understand this, and they have incorporated play into the workday. Some technology companies give employees a percentage of the day to do what they want, which includes working on their own ideas and even playing. Parts of the Google campus resemble a grown-up kid's playhouse, with video games, Tinkertoys, Ping-Pong tables, treadmills, massages, and free food. Many Googlers come to the office (they can work from home) because they *want* to, not because they have to.

> **A big reason to play at work is to manage fear.**

Leading with Humor

Not many companies can provide what Google does, but I can't count how many times I've been on working groups or teams that have found the solution to a problem while out to dinner or clowning around in the ready room.

In a study, Northwestern University researchers asked three different groups of college students to solve word association puzzles after each group watched a short video of a funny, scary, or boring situation, respectively. The students who watched the funny video solved more of the puzzles overall, and significantly more by sudden insight, than those who'd seen the scary or boring video beforehand ("Tracing the Spark of Creative Problem-Solving," *New York Times*, December 6, 2010).

It doesn't take PhDs to understand that the environment we create determines how well we innovate and solve problems.

Rock On! Physical Energy Helps Too.

Music and exercise help to put me in the right frame of mind. When I'm writing, I listen to the rhythms of Cajun and Zydeco. When I'm preparing to go on missions, I don't listen to Barry White. I bring on the AC/DC! I love both, but each puts me in a different state of mind—one makes me want to dance, while the other revs me up and gets the adrenalin pumping!

I also believe in the power of physical movement to get the brain working. I have often done walk-and-talk meetings and have found solutions that way. Others prefer to stand, rather than sit, at their specially modified desks to keep both the body and the brain focused and active.

Embrace the Suck

Organizations that have a shared First, Fast, Fearless consciousness can laugh during the hard times and not allow the fear to take control. Laughter in the face of adversity creates an offensive mindset. We encourage BUD/S students not only

(continued)

> to sing in the freezing water to create ersatz motivation but also to laugh during pain and to "embrace the suck."
>
> If you embrace the suck and approach the problem—whether it's an underperforming employee, a defective product, or an aggressive competitor—with a dose of humor mixed in with mental toughness, you're more likely to come away a winner.

What Makes Innovation Tick?

Einstein once said, "If at first, the idea is not absurd, then there is no hope for it." One thing SEALs do better than any other force I've seen or been with is to innovate, or as we say, "Make shit up."

As leaders, the environment we create determines how well people can think outside the box. For SEALs, when our lives are on the line, innovation is like leadership. It's not a part-time exercise. It's a way of life. When our lives are at stake, we must be willing to hear—and try—"stupid" ideas to find a creative solution to get ourselves out of trouble, survive, and ultimately, win.

> **Innovation is like leadership.**
> **It's not a part-time job. It's a way of life.**

Be Willing to Change; Be Willing to *Accept* Change

For years in the SEAL Teams, we had an established way of making direct action assaults in an urban environment. This sequence of tactics, techniques, and procedures (TTPs) had been around for a long time; we seldom changed it. When the Iraq and Afghanistan wars began, we found ourselves quickly learning the real-world deficiencies of our TTPs. Instead of entering buildings to rescue hostages, we were going in to get terrorists and others who don't care about lives—including their own.

It didn't take too many of our people getting shot in the face for innovation to kick in. We quickly developed new TTPs to put our enemies on the defensive. Our lives depended on our changing what we had always done. It's no different in the market when a major technology shift occurs. If you don't adapt to the new conditions, you might find yourself out of business.

As a leader, these kinds of decisions are hard, but if you establish the right conditions for teams to innovate and come up with new ideas, it can happen. If you allow people to take risks and solve problems, it can happen. And if your teams aren't scared of what's *inside* the perimeter, it can happen.

Be Willing to Go Big

Sometimes legacies, experiences, and the beliefs created by both can be the worst things for an organization. This may sound counterintuitive. We are proud of our legacy and value our experience, but legacy and experience can also make you less open to new ideas. "You can't teach an old dog new tricks," as the saying goes. Creative thinking requires moving beyond the constraints of our legacy and experience.

Before 2005, SEALs never imagined we'd be engaged in combat advising and Foreign Internal Defense (FID) operations. Our Green Beret brothers did this, "not us." We always saw ourselves living in the shadows, blowing off doors in the middle of the night, and hunting the enemy on small specialized operations. But FID operations were critical in the war to winning western Iraq. We knew that we had to do everything we could to, in line with our ethos, "bring the full spectrum of combat power to bear to achieve [the] mission and the goals established by [our] country."

There was no playbook, so we "made shit up" as we went along. With the invaluable wisdom and counsel from a Green

Beret Colonel, I guided the unit to figure out how to be a "force multiplier," a term we use when we embed with other forces to lead and train them during missions. We would have 4 SEALs leading 200 Iraqis to maximize combat power and abilities. Nothing was off the table; I was open to all ideas.

Think Differently and Win

I asked the troops to find the solution to maximize our abilities. Within a short time, they came back with a plan that didn't just require a minor rudder correction. It was in a different ocean! And it was good because they had been out getting situational awareness, and they had seen the actual need on the battlefield. In the meantime, the ideas coming down from the top were about as useful as football bats. Grounded in theory alone, I'm sure they all sounded great in a staff meeting room.

The troops saw that, for us to develop a highly skilled unit, the larger Iraqi unit of 1,500 needed to be in sync. They came up with a plan not only to train this specialized unit but also to take on an advisor role with the larger Iraqi brigade. We had never done anything like this before. It wasn't just "outside our paradigm." It was somewhere else altogether. For most SEALs, it was unimaginable at this point in the war. To be honest, most didn't want to do it. But I had some great leaders and thinkers working for me, who understood it and supported it.

We put together a plan and sent it up the chain of command for approval, expecting some serious pushback. Thankfully, my boss realized that although we were taking a big leap from what we had done before, it was what was necessary, so he approved the plan.

The impact was amazing. We ran multiple missions around the clock (which made SEALs happy) and made much faster progress! A few months after I returned from this deployment, national news outlets broadcast a ceremony of the troops we had advised taking official ownership of their own battle space, and ultimately, their lives.

A Mickey Mouse Idea

I took heavy criticism from various members of the SEAL community, especially from the Cold War generation. They believed that we operated only "in the shadows" and there we should remain. At times, I feared being relieved of command following heated discussions with my superiors.

But my motto—and what I said to them often—was, "I'll dress up like Mickey Mouse and hand out soccer balls if that's what it takes. Mission first!" We went big because that's what was required to win western Iraq. Leaders have to be ready to make giant leaps. Course corrections won't always suffice.

"I Already Know What I Know"

When people ask Ken Blanchard why he coauthors books with other people, he answers, "Well, I already know what I know." Ken values new ideas and different perspectives on an issue. It's one of the keys to his success.

Everyone has unique life experiences. That's why I believe so strongly in leaders being learners. The more you learn, the more diversified your thinking becomes—and the greater your ability to see problems differently.

Ignorance is dangerous in all aspects of life and leadership. Combine ignorance with arrogance, and the result can be devastating.

Your Strongest Trait Can Be Your Worst Enemy

As part of the continuous training cycle, every SEAL returns multiple times to a shooting range located in the southern United States. On that range, there are two buildings we refer to as "kill houses," where you shoot live bullets into targets throughout the structure. The walls at this particular location are "ballistic," meaning they are able to stop bullets from penetrating the walls into the next room. Unfortunately, one day, a bullet went through the wall and killed a Navy SEAL.

I was the investigating officer for this death. One of my first duties was to interview every person in the kill house that day. Those interviews revealed a pattern clear as day.

We usually get it right on the SEAL Teams, but an occasional mistake can be lethal. Every SEAL who had previously been to this shooting range had 100 percent confidence in the ability of the walls to stop bullets. Why? Because those walls had always done so in the past.

That said, every new SEAL was apprehensive about being behind those walls. They were unsure enough about it that they held a "new guy" meeting to discuss the safety of the walls. But here's where our strength became the enemy: SEALs value courage, so they didn't want to express their concerns. They didn't want to look afraid; they didn't want the shame. I don't blame them at all.

All the rookies saw the danger, while none of the veterans did. When problem solving, it's important to get a fresh set of eyes on the situation and make sure you keep the fear outside the perimeter. The new SEALs were scared to bring up their fears of the wall. Somehow the team didn't make them feel safe enough to say something without being shamed or ridiculed. (Notably, there's a lot of pressure on new guys to perform. We always tell them to bring up safety issues, but sometimes SEALs barely past the new guy stage put enough pressure on them to silence them. It's part of the subculture we work hard to eliminate.)

As with most things, embracing diverse opinions and having an unbiased view are of great value. SEAL Teams cross-train with other services of the U.S. military and other countries as much as we can. We always learn something that helps us be better.

It's part of the First, Fast, Fearless mindset.

TAKEAWAYS

- Leading with humor shows humility. People respect humble leaders and feel safer within the brotherhood.

- Because of your authority, subordinates can be hypersensitive to your remarks. Don't lead with your ego. Self-deprecation works best.

- Enough of the right kind of humor or "play" can help the team be innovative and at its best.

- Fear inhibits the brain's executive functions, hindering reasoning, attention, problem solving, and mental flexibility, among other things.

- Laughter in the face of adversity shows an offensive mindset.

- When our lives are on the line, we must be willing to embrace "stupid" ideas to survive and, ultimately, win.

- Innovation, like leadership, is not a part-time job. It's a way of life.

- Be willing to accept change, be willing to go big, and be willing to think differently.

- Don't let the past paradigm lure you into complacency. An "I know what I know" attitude can be destructive to innovation, not to mention, dangerous.

- Embrace diversity—and embrace diversity of thinking. You'll learn something to help you be better.

CHAPTER 18

Thriving on the Rhythm: Seizing First, Fast, Fearless Leadership Moments

Silence is worse: all truths that are kept silent become poisonous.
—FRIEDRICH NIETZSCHE

The cook assigned to my unit in Iraq was less than a year away from full retirement from the Navy. He had never been to war, and he was quite honest in his wish not to go. Reluctant though he was, he went. In the military, we don't give invitations. We give orders. Before he showed up, I had heard that he had fought tooth and nail not to have to go. I knew this situation was bound to provide a leadership moment.

Upon his arrival, I immediately brought him into my office and thanked him for coming on such short notice. I told him I empathized with his situation.

The cook had been working in Naval Special Warfare for a few years. All he knew was that SEALs ate more food than he thought humanly possible. He felt transparent around them. I wanted him to understand the mission and what these "ungrateful" SEALs were really out there doing.

So one evening, I invited him to sit in and listen to a mission brief we were conducting later that night. Normally, only operators come to these briefs, but I decided to bring him in to see what goes on while everyone else in camp is sleeping. Not only did the "light come on" but he also came to understand the importance of what we did and the sacrifices those "ungrateful" SEALs made every night. He became one of the best and most motivated team members I had. I also found out that he was quite the carpenter, so during his downtime, he would take on important construction projects. He was all in.

It wasn't long before I brought in someone from each department to listen to the briefs. Quickly, we found that just by being in the same room and hearing things for themselves, the larger team understood what we needed and how they could contribute. I learned that compartmentalizing people according to their functions is not good for the mission. We also realized that group diversity stimulated greater innovative thinking.

At this juncture in the Iraq War, the turrets on top of our armored vehicles had huge gaps in them. Those gaps didn't give our operators a warm fuzzy feeling; they were inadequate for the threat level. During one of the briefs, the guys joked about being a turret gunner with our heads and upper bodies exposed, protected only by a piece of equipment made by the lowest bidder. One of our support personnel heard this, and a few days later, the support folks had built something we called "the pope turret." The pope turret covered the gunner with ballistic glass 360 degrees around, minimizing the threat of getting hit.

Why do I share this story? Not because I want to describe a new piece of military technology or the military need that led to its development. I'm more interested in the context—that is, the situation—in which good leadership forged, out of raw iron, a team spirit, a willingness to help each other, and an ability to innovate on the ground without the usual bureaucracy, rules, and processes in place to impair progress. This is an example of First, Fast, Fearless leadership,

Get your teams in rhythm, and seize important leadership moments to keep them there.

Leadership in the Moment

Even though I've practiced it often through the years, I've never been very good at meditation. Like many, I find that I can silence the voice inside my head for only a few seconds.

One of the few times the voice goes away and I find myself living purely in the moment is when I am working with great teams, especially in combat. Sneaking up to a building and waiting for everyone to get set for a "direct action" offensive assault was very much like that. In those moments, I didn't regret the past or worry about the future. I was fully in the present and at my best. Each of my senses was heightened and engaged to absorb as much information as possible. It was a trance-like, time-warped state of being, and I was truly in my rhythm.

In my experience, time moves effortlessly when a team finally gets its rhythm. It doesn't mean the job is easy—in fact, if the leaders set up the right conditions for the team to thrive, sometimes, the harder the job, the better the rhythm. Just as people often value and cherish the hard-won victories or accomplishments that took a great deal of effort, SEALs reflect back on their BUD/S training with fondness and reverence. The important and worthwhile things are often the hardest to do—and the most rewarding. Why else would we go to the moon or climb Mount Everest? When I set up a team, people know up front that I have high expectations of the team—and of myself. It won't be easy—and they wouldn't want it to be.

> If leaders set up the right conditions for the team to thrive, the harder the job, the better the rhythm.

Goldilocks Expectations:
Not Too Hard, Not Too Easy

In the third week of BUD/S training, we do what we call a "run by the podium." Typically, we start soft sand runs at the instructor podium just behind the BUD/S compound on Coronado Beach. We run down the beach, turn around, and run back to the podium.

But on this particular run, we go to the podium and keep right on going! Almost all the students fall way behind the instructors as we keep the same pace. Their expectations are broken and with it, their will to continue. (Keep in mind that at this point, the SEAL recruits are new, and they haven't yet learned not to give up. We are still in the selection phase.)

We would measure the heart rate of the students who fell behind. Without fail, they were way below their anaerobic threshold. They were physically fine, but they were beaten mentally. As a leader, it's important to set clear expectations up front so that teams don't have to run past the podium and have their will broken.

Don't make it too easy or too hard. A little unexpected adversity is OK, even beneficial, but don't make it so hard as to break their spirit or make it so easy as to be dull.

> **Not too hard, not too easy.**
> **Set expectations to be challenging but**
> **not over the top.**

Avoiding a Culture of Secrecy

Prior to 9/11, there was a culture of secrecy across the government. Almost all agencies kept information and intelligence to themselves. In some cases, agencies intentionally kept information from other parts of the government—to maintain control, stay within charter, or "compete." In so doing, they were more concerned with their own well-being than that of their nation or the greater mission. Worse, it led to the emergence of conspiracy theories. When people don't know what's going on, they assume the worst.

Quickly and tragically, 9/11 proved that had to change. We had to share information. We had to take a bit more risk that information may be compromised. Our government developed "fusion centers," in which all parts of the intelligence world came together and shared information up and down the chain of command.

On my micro level, SEALs and other Special Forces had to develop this mentality as well. The days of living in the shadows and segregating ourselves from the conventional military were over. We soon discovered that we could learn a great deal just by being in the same room as others; people will surprise you. The lesson holds in the business world: don't hold too much "close to the chest." Not only will you deny yourself access to new ideas and perspectives but you will also encounter gridlock when you have to move fast.

> Secrecy and silos will cause you to miss
> out on good ideas.
> They will also cause you to stumble
> when you have to move fast.

From Silos to Shared Consciousness

We began to hold "fusing" meetings of our own within Special Operations, and we have continued this practice. We run video teleconferences hosted by leadership across the globe. We open up access to these conferences so people can hear and see for themselves—from their leaders—what's going on several levels above them. Participation is limited, but it's still an incredible tool for team members to get situational awareness and develop the shared consciousness of the mission. It takes courage for leaders to be this open because, for some, controlling information is a way of wielding power. But as we know by now, First, Fast, Fearless leaders rely on power by example.

Like all of our meetings, SEAL Team fusion meetings have Rules of Engagement (ROE) that govern the flow of the meeting. Time is crucial, so meetings are run like operations—on time and on target. These meetings should have a rhythm too, as well as an economy of effort.

Making Intentions Clear, in Your Own Words

To lead at the speed of war, one must share information both *up* and *down* the chain of command. Furthermore, the *intentions behind* leaders' orders must be clear. When we first began to advise the Iraqis about combat, we were given orders not to run missions unilaterally. We had to run them together with the Iraqis. We developed a great mission statement, but the mission statement wasn't enough.

In the beginning, one of my officers came up and asked in a frustrated tone, "How many Iraqis do we have to take on the mission tonight?" This question seemed fair enough, but I realized that he didn't understand the intent of our mission. As a leader, I knew I hadn't made that clear, and I needed to do so immediately because if the officer didn't know the mission intent, then his team wouldn't either.

I spent that night coming up with a clear "leader's intent" statement to put the mission in context for the operators. A statement of intent isn't a restatement of the mission. It is a statement, in your own language, about what must happen for the mission to succeed and what the end state looks like.

In the world of VUCA, unanticipated situations and opportunities arise, requiring your subordinates to exercise their own initiative. If they are clear on what winning looks like, they can use their discretion and make decisions that support the mission. Making the leader's intent loud and clear empowers your people.

When my officer asked me how many Iraqis we had to take, my answer was, "As many as we can," because the mission was to transition the Iraqis into taking over the fight while we transitioned out of it. Americans had taken heavy casualties in these streets; the intent was to stop that and to enable the Iraqis to fight for their own country.

> As a leader, make your *intentions* clear, and others will *want to*, and *be able to*, follow.

A Three-Part Statement of the Leader's Intent

An effective expression of the leader's intent usually has three parts: purpose, key tasks, and end state; appropriate guidance; and priorities.

Purpose, Key Tasks, End State

We try to add a statement of the leader's intent whenever we task someone to do something important. It can be made formally or informally. It's a clear and concise statement of what subordinates must do to succeed and achieve the desired end state in the environment they're in. It gives subordinates enough context to exercise initiative when unanticipated opportunities or constraints arise or when the plan they are executing is no longer relevant. The leader's intent is not a restatement of the mission. It provides a broader purpose, one that helps put things in a clearer context. It is written in your own words, not as it comes down from command. I present the big picture, so people get a better sense of why they are doing what they are doing.

Over the years, I've found that most leaders don't really know how to delegate. Delegation isn't about making assignments of tasks and duties. It's a proactive event, requiring leaders to be very clear about their intent and the intended outcome. Like everything we do, delegation is an offensive action.

The second part of a statement of intent deals with key tasks and constraints: specific items that must be done along the way, keeping a budget, meeting a deadline. Note that these tasks aren't tied to a particular concept of operation, but rather, they define the parameters for mission success. Mission success is the end game you're looking to achieve. The leader's statement of intent isn't a "fire and forget" action. It is a living document. When the enemy votes, we may have to revisit our intent and share the changes with our people.

It isn't just a vision statement. Rather, it usually suggests some intermediate steps, and it may be revised multiple times, as needed, within whatever time frame necessary. Sometimes it just illuminates specs, boundaries, and tasks that need to be done for success. The focus on the end state is key—as in when I stated the intent for the Iraqis to take over the fight and to own the mission when we left. The end state is a clear picture of what success will look like.

Ultimately, the better the team understands the mission and intent, the better equipped and empowered it will be to execute. But it only works in an ethos-based organization where individuals can be trusted to do the right thing.

> **Delegation isn't about making assignments.
> It's about sharing an intended outcome.**

Keeping Your Middle Managers in the Loop Too

Another key part of this idea is the importance of informing all your staff of your intent. In larger organizations, information is cascaded down to the people through staff or middle managers. A gap in the understanding of your intent can lead to misguided action and introduce unnecessary bureaucracy.

In the military, leaders must be replaceable because you never know when an enemy vote might take a leader out of the fight. In business, you don't typically lose leaders this way! But leaders may take new jobs, they may be deployed on something else, or they may not be available for some reason. The organization must be able to move according to the original intent.

A Small Dose of Guidance

For more complex assignments, the leader should provide some guidance toward the solution. The situation will likely dictate the degree of guidance needed. Given at the beginning, this guidance should serve to get—and keep—people working in the right direction. It will help get things done more efficiently.

But I should be clear: it isn't about telling your people how to do something. Rather, it's about providing the necessary information to arrive at a solution. Your job as a leader is to decide how much and what kind of guidance will get it done.

Priorities

Prioritizing team efforts is a central and critical part of being a good team leader. We SEALs call it "rack and stack." In practice, good prioritizing tends to be difficult; many leaders believe *everything* is important, which means that nothing is important!

Once I had a boss who was notorious for being what we call a "staff Nazi." He had an aversion to prioritizing. At the time, we said, "He didn't care about the mule; he just loaded the wagon." Even though it's difficult to tell your boss that you can't do everything, you still need to request guidance on what takes priority. Good leaders embrace this and can rank their priorities, accepting that some of the tasks may not be done.

At the time, I was the Training Officer for the West Coast SEAL Teams. We were many years into the wars in Iraq and Afghanistan. Manning for staff positions took a backseat to positions in the war zones. We had no more than a skeleton crew in all of our commands throughout the organization.

During the first six months I worked for him, the staff Nazi never consolidated what we were all working on. He was known for "hallway tasking," so we stayed out of the hallways as much as possible! He didn't have a holistic approach. He gave fire-and-forget tasks, over and over again, at random, loading up the wagon. It wasn't until he became frustrated for what he thought was a lack of staff progress that we put together an update brief to show him what we were doing and how far along we were.

As the Training and Readiness Officer, I took on the biggest piece of the brief. I calculated that I had been given some 107 tasks to complete. Not all could be accomplished overnight. Some were major projects that required months to get in place. At this time, my team was two people deep, including me. Being a good follower, I told the boss up front that I was looking for guidance on his priorities, and I began to go through all the tasks that he had assigned. About an hour or so in, he gave up and called off the briefing. I reiterated my request for his priorities so we could get something done. He refused to give me an answer and continued to complain about the inadequacies of his staff, which as we know, is never acceptable. You play the hand you're dealt and make the best of it.

I understand that prioritizing is hard, especially when resources are limited, but leaders must have the courage to set the priorities for their people *and* communicate them both up and down the chain of command.

Becoming a Learning Organization: The After Action Review

In the SEAL Teams, we understand that our mistakes might be written in blood, so it's important not to repeat them. When you're dealing in life and death, being honest is imperative. We cannot allow arrogance to blind us to our limitations. We "train to failure" to learn the perimeter of our capabilities. Humility is key to having an honest organization, an organization that faces the cold hard facts of reality.

After almost everything we do, we religiously perform an After Action Review (AAR). For example, after every run through the kill house, practicing target assaults on structures, we stop to debrief to reinforce positive behavior and to spot what needs to be corrected. More formal AARs are also done after each SEAL Team deployment. We bring different members of the organization together to share lessons learned and to implement any changes to the processes.

An AAR Checklist

A learning organization requires honesty and openness, without finger-pointing and faultfinding. All failures come with a cost, so it's critical for great organizations to capture the mistakes, understand them, and make course corrections. Our AARs, whether formal or informal, are conducted in a nonthreatening way. The process, which is guided by a set of questions, is simple and clear:

- What did we intend to do?
- What happened?
- What went wrong?
- What went right?
- What do we have to fix?

Everyone is part of this process. We all know to leave our egos at the door to objectively assess what happened and what did and didn't work. Mistakes, while unfortunate, often give us the clearest and most useful opportunity for self-examination. We can do dozens of direct action missions and think everything is perfect until something goes south and we find a hole in our tactics. After such failures, it's critical to capture the lessons because they can be very expensive, both to resources and morale.

Prior to SEAL Team deployments, the whole team (also referred to as a *squadron*) would do a "final battle problem," or exercise, in which all 400 to 500 SEALs and support personnel would deploy to a remote area to set up our combat systems. We would run them through elaborate scenarios to mimic the chaos in war for both staff and operators. After this week-long exercise, an extensive AAR would help the Commanding Officers make last-minute corrections before going to war. All hands were on deck for this AAR, including the Commanding Officers. A strong and safe perimeter within the organization is critical for a successful AAR.

Bringing AARs into Your Workplace

To my knowledge, business organizations don't do AARs frequently enough. And when they do conduct an AAR, the process often takes the form of the annual performance review. In which case, the AAR becomes too personal—more about the individual than the process. By that time, the issues may have escalated, or the memories may have faded. Reviews can be uncomfortable when they are not part of a daily practice.

Organizations that conduct regular "war room" meetings when solving problems come closest to capturing the spirit of this idea. I recommend frequent and objective AARs for all teams and organizations, even when they are not in a war room situation.

It's all part of First, Fast, Fearless leadership.

TAKEAWAYS

- Not too easy, not too hard. Set expectations to be challenging and clear.

- First, Fast, Fearless leaders rely on openness and team play, not power, to be effective.

- To lead at the speed of war, you need to share information both up and down the chain of command, as well as sideways across silos.

- As a leader, make your *intent* clear, and others will want to—and be able to—follow.

- Delegation is about sharing an intended outcome, and it is an offensive action.

- It's important for everyone to understand the leader's intent so that the mission can proceed in the absence of the leader, whether she or he is taken out by enemy votes or by organizational change.

- The statement of the leader's intent should include:

  - Purpose, key tasks, end state

  - Appropriate guidance

  - Priorities

- Guidance isn't telling your people how to do something. It's about providing the necessary information to arrive at a solution.

- Relatively frequent After Action Reviews (AARs) capture lessons and enable course corrections, improving both performance and morale.

CHAPTER 19

The Man in the Arena

On the surface, shooting, just like leading, seems simple enough, but when your life and livelihood depend on it, you can never get too good at it. What do I mean by that? Simply, to shoot and miss accomplishes nothing. It is wasteful and may provide a false sense of security. The SEAL expression is: "You can't miss fast enough to win a gunfight."

An effective organization must thrive on its leadership and strive to get things right the *first* time, *every* time, *all of* the time. How do you make First, Fast, Fearless leadership a way of life?

Focus on the Front Sight

"Front sight focus" is another SEAL expression, which reveals a great deal about how we approach the art of shooting. It means focusing on the front sight of your weapon when you want to hit the target. For a pistol, that's about three feet in front of you (including your arm length).

The target itself is blurred because your eye can focus on only one distance at a time, much like a camera. To most new shooters, this is counterintuitive; they want to focus on the target. Old shooters understand this as a critical piece of mastering shooting. The farther away the target, the more critical is front sight focus. A little blur on the front sight at three feet grows exponentially with the distance of the shot.

It's the same in business. If you focus too much on the bottom line—and lead accordingly—you may miss your target. Leaders should keep people focused on the front sight post to ultimately hit the target. The trick is to see and know the target, but to focus on the key steps—the sight posts—to get there. Focusing on the front sight means focusing on the smaller, doable parts of the job, which ultimately reduces fear.

Mastering a weapon, such as a pistol, requires only a handful of skills, but to be a great shooter, you must perform each of them perfectly every time. Leading is the same way: you must constantly monitor the fundamentals and assess the situation to do the right things that will enable you to hit the target. You can't force a bullet into a bull's-eye, nor can you force a team to excel. Hitting the target is the result of great leadership.

> **Front sight focus reduces fear by focusing on smaller, doable parts of the job.**

Train to Failure—Not to Fail

You might be the greatest company or military in the world, but that's not good enough. You still must win.

In the SEAL world, we "train ourselves to failure, but not to fail." We push ourselves to tackle bigger problems than we can handle. Even when outgunned and surrounded, we never allow ourselves to quit. We keep fighting through the problem. We hit the point of failure—physical exhaustion, low ammunition, compromised position—but we don't ever lie down. We keep fighting until we win. We don't practice losing. This prepares us to keep fighting and feel like we can win even in the worst combat situations.

The idea is to push yourself—to stretch to the point of failure. You aren't in business to feel good. You are there to hit the target; that's the goal. Good teams can achieve this, and they are better suited to reach the brink of failure—and then succeed, together.

Don't Look Around. Make It Happen.

When giving an order for which we expect 100 percent commitment to doing everything possible to get the job done, we say, "Make it happen." We teach and enforce this from the beginning of training and throughout our careers. It tells the team members to do whatever possible to accomplish the mission at hand— and that they have the discretion and flexibility to make the necessary adjustments with the resources available. It's a powerful force that can unleash the invisible efforts that only the person doing the job knows are possible. Giving such an order breeds accountability, and accountability breeds extreme ownership of the outcome.

> "Make it happen" breeds accountability,
> and accountability makes it happen.

If you lead with a strong ethos, including humility and sacrifice for your people, you empower your team to achieve the inconceivable.

The Man in the Arena

The SEAL experience has been one of great reward and, occasionally, great struggle. Years ago, before a difficult deployment, my best friend, Matt, handed me an excerpt of a speech entitled

"Citizenship in a Republic," given by President Theodore Roosevelt at the Sorbonne in Paris, France, on April 23, 1910:

> It is not the critic who counts; not the man who points out how the strong man stumbles, or where the doer of deeds could have done them better. The credit belongs to the man who is actually in the arena, whose face is marred by dust and sweat and blood; who strives valiantly; who errs, who comes short again and again, because there is no effort without error and shortcoming; but who does actually strive to do the deeds; who knows great enthusiasms, the great devotions; who spends himself in a worthy cause; who at the best knows in the end the triumph of high achievement, and who at the worst, if he fails, at least fails while daring greatly, so that his place shall never be with those cold and timid souls who neither know victory nor defeat.

It's been in the front of my notebook ever since. I also have those words on a gold plaque in my living room, and they are displayed with the tattered American flag I flew under my command in Iraq.

When you accept the responsibility of—and the accountability that comes with—leadership, there will be hard times. But remember, it's not the critic who counts. It's the man who is actually in the arena. If you cultivate the brand of a true leader, build and love your brotherhood, and set the conditions for your people to thrive, there will be great rewards.

Step into the arena. Dare greatly!

First, Fast, Fearless Leadership Maxims

A mercenary does a job because he's paid to. A soldier does his because he's ordered to. A warrior does it because he *wants* to.

One's training is never complete.

"Leadership is getting people to want to do, and to be able to do, something important." —Peter Sander, *What Will Steve Jobs Do?*

When leadership is right, you don't see it anymore.

Be the cause, not the effect.

Leaders present in times of stress are far more valued than ones who stop by once in a while when things are going well.

A first strike mindset is the path to action. Action is the antidote to stress and fear.

Offensive thinkers don't dwell on their pain or the unfairness in their lives.

An ethos is *your* Declaration of Independence. It is your guiding light.

Without an ethos, you might become trapped in a mythos.

Having a strong ethos can transform organizations and change people's lives.

Your work should be your temple—it's a chance to express your humanity.

Eliminate I, me, and mine.

The higher you go, the less you know, the more you owe.

Leadership is something you do *with* people, not *to* them.

Tell people what they did right. It's a humbling experience.

At the highest level, we are servant leaders. Everything else is just smoke.

When people are scared of their leadership, they spend most of their time managing leadership's perception of them.

As a leader, I see myself as a playful sheepdog—but ready to take on the wolf.

Go see your subordinates. Don't always expect them to come see you.

Mutual respect and dignity spark the spirit of leadership and compassion.

Leadership is not one thing you do. It's *everything* you do.

You build it and they will come. Leaders don't just lead. They build a following.

Personal discipline is a great leadership tool. If you're sloppy and unprepared, people will notice and judge you accordingly.

Leadership occurs in concentric rings. What you do as a leader resonates throughout the organization.

Be in the moment during times of stress.

Everyone who wants to be a leader should be there in times of adversity.

In stressful conditions, people are hypersensitive to leadership.

Once your see leadership, you always see it.

Good leaders evaluate what's going on with all six senses before they step in. Their sixth sense is their personal experience.

Great leaders are great listeners and can hear—or sense—people's fears. Anger, resentment, and frustration are all symptoms of fear.

When listening to someone, don't get distracted by phones, computers, or visitors. Shut the door or find a quiet place. Otherwise, you'll waste your time and theirs.

Never disrespect people personally or publicly. If you do, apologize quickly.

When complimenting someone or approving something, don't use the words *but* or *however*. You're probably looking for perfection in things that don't matter.

Charisma is the opposite of ego.

Never focus on getting dealt a better hand.

Dealing with limited resources—and getting things done anyway—is a sign of accountability.

A lack of accountability leads to excuses, and excuses slow down the organization.

Accountability and authority must travel together.

History won't remember your excuses.

Blame is much like fear: it is highly contagious.

We bend the rules. We don't break them. Mission first.

You cannot move at the speed of war when you are caught up in the rules of bureaucracy.

There is no rule book for innovation and creativity. If there were, it would be obsolete instantly.

You manage things, but you lead people.

If you have the right values and mission, the goals and metrics tend to take care of themselves.

Be driven by values and missions, not goals.

Their time is just as important—if not more so—than yours.

Gain respect the old-fashioned way. *Earn it*. Never resort to fear.

Find the dominant talents. Turn them into respect and trust.

Without an ethos, the outcome of moral decisions can vary greatly.

As a leader, you should expect mistakes with expertise, knowledge, and experience, but values-based mistakes should be dealt with swiftly and not allowed.

Sacrifice as much as or more than you expect of your teams.

Do what you expect your teams to do, and know what you expect your teams to know.

Swim buddies get everyone across the finish line faster.

If you want teams to be accountable, hold them accountable for each other.

Most successful people have a swim buddy.

A swim buddy doesn't always share the spotlight. He or she may work in the background.

Swim buddies don't cost a dime.

The quality of leadership can ignite or destroy a team.

When your rhythm resonates, it creates momentum; other processes fall in line.

A team *moving forward together* has more credibility than a band of individuals.

Your worst enemies may lie inside your perimeter. They are often more destructive.

If you cannot shame a teammate, you probably can't trust him either.

As a leader, you must deal with toxic behavior. Not dealing with it erodes team confidence in you.

Having the wrong person is always worse than having one less person.

Don't put a Band-Aid on gangrene.

Your brand as follower—not just leader—is also important.

A follower owns the decision too.

There are no bad teams—only bad leaders.

"My way or the highway" destroys followership—and teamwork eventually.

Following is just leading from a different direction.

Good leadership + good followership = trust + brotherhood

Walk the talk, and never leave anyone behind.

Don't manage. Lead. *Especially* when times are tough.

Take care of them even after they leave. The rest of the team will take note.

If you leave them behind, they will leave *you* behind. It's a little like love.

Leading at the speed of war is based on well-orchestrated values, teamwork, and timing. When it works, it creates music.

In the marketplace, the enemy is almost always voting and seldom sits still.

A values-driven team with established trust is fertile ground for delegation.

If you start to smell fresh paint everywhere, you're probably not getting the truth.

Nix the fancy PowerPoints. At the end of the day, they may only reflect your insecurity.

If you want people to be winners, treat them like winners.

A meaningful appraisal shows as much humility as an authentic apology.

Our profession, like most professions, is too serious to take too seriously.

A big reason to play at work is to manage fear.

Innovation is like leadership. It's not a part-time job. It's a way of life.

If leaders set up the right conditions for the team to thrive, the harder the job, the better the rhythm.

Not too hard, not too easy. Set expectations to be challenging but not over the top.

Secrecy and silos will cause you to miss out on good ideas. They will also cause you to stumble when you have to move fast.

As a leader, make your *intentions* clear, and others will *want to*, and *be able to*, follow.

Delegation isn't about making assignments. It's about sharing an intended outcome.

Front sight focus reduces fear by focusing on smaller, doable parts of the job.

"Make it happen" breeds accountability, and accountability makes it happen.

Index

Enemies within perimeter, 181–184
Energy, channeling, 46
Epictetus, 35
"Essentials of Servant Leadership"
    (Greenleaf), 39
Ethos, 55–69
    constructing your own, 66–69
    crafting of, 59–61
    Declaration of Independence
        as, 55
    definition of, 56
    implementation of, 62–63
    leading with rules vs., 131–132
    mindset for creating, 63–66
    moral guidance from, 147–148
    mythos vs., 58–59
    and vision, 134–135
    (See also SEAL Ethos)
Ethos conference (San Clemente
    Island), 59–62
Excuses, making, 115–116
Executive system (brain), 236
Expectations, 68–69, 248
Experience, innovation and, 239–240
External trust, building, 152–153

Failure, training to, 260–261
False motivation, 175–176
Fast roping, 142
Fatal funnel, 26
Fear:
    and brain, 4–5, 236
    courage/action from, 44–49
    and effectiveness of leaders, 108
    and insecurity, 77
    love as opposite of, 78, 216
    and respect, 146
    servant leadership as antidote for,
        78–79
    of shame, 184
    and swim buddies, 157–158
    and VUCA, 40

Feedback:
    from followers, 202–203
    giving, 105–107
    and humility, 80–82
    SEAL caricature skit as, 76
Field craft, 99–101
Final battle problem, 256
Fiorina, Carleton "Carly," 164
Firing, 110–111, 190–191
First strike mindset, 43–53
    adopting, 47–48
    example of, 48–49
    and focus, 45–46
    and playing offense, 49–52
    and reputation, 90
    of SEALs, 43–44
    and stress, 52–53
    and turning fear/VUCA into
        courage/action, 44–49
    value of adopting a, 46–47
First-line step, 31
Fit, organizational, 201–202
Five pillars of leadership, 34–40,
    135–138
Focus, 45–46, 259–260
Follower, being a good, 199–203
Followership, 193–203
    and being a good follower,
        199–203
    and building a following, 89–90
    and leadership, 195–196, 199
    and letting your people be the
        winners, 196–199
Force multipliers, 240
Ford, Gerald, 36
Ford Motor Company, 58
Foreign Internal Defense (FID)
    operations, 193–194, 239–240
Fortified compounds, leaving, 224
Frankl, Viktor, 233
Freefall jumping, 24
Fresh paint, smell of, 225–226

About the Author

Ed Hiner is a genuine hero of the global war on terrorism. In his 20-year career as a Navy SEAL, he made nine major deployments on five continents, half of which were combat tours. Twice awarded the Bronze Star with V for valor and combat leadership, Hiner commanded hundreds of direct combat missions and low visibility operations in Iraq, Afghanistan, Southeast Asia, and Central America.

Born and raised in Virginia's Blue Ridge Mountains, Hiner grew up with a thirst for competition, and he developed an indomitable will to win that would serve him well in his life's work as a warrior and leader. His baseball talent earned him a scholarship to Virginia Commonwealth University. During a holiday break from college in Virginia Beach, Hiner spent a day helping out a Navy wife who was being forced from her home while her husband was deployed to the Persian Gulf. On a trip to her storage unit, Hiner met an active duty Navy SEAL who volunteered to help. The ensuing day-long conversation provided Hiner (who had never heard of the SEALs) with the spark he needed. He hitchhiked back to Richmond, went straight to the U.S. Navy recruiter, and enlisted.

Hiner graduated from the Basic Underwater Demolition/SEAL (BUD/S) training in 1993 with class 189. Prior to the terrorist attacks of September 11, 2001, he deployed several times as an enlisted SEAL Operator. He was then picked to attend Officer Candidate School where he earned his commission as a distinguished honor graduate and class president. Following that, Hiner earned a master's degree in executive leadership from the University of San Diego. He went on to make numerous deployments as a SEAL Officer.

Shortly after 9/11, Hiner was selected to integrate directly into an elite unit of the British Special Forces, where he served as Executive Officer and team member of a highly classified Task Force at the height of the Iraq War and follow-on counterinsurgency efforts. For his efforts while serving in this classified Task Force, Hiner was specially promoted to Lieutenant Commander and given command of his own SEAL Task Unit, which deployed to Ramadi at the peak of the Iraq insurgency. This was the first time in the history of the SEAL Teams that a Lieutenant was promoted to Lieutenant Commander for the express purpose of leading a specific combat deployment.

Throughout his SEAL career, Hiner felt it imperative that he continually pass along what he had learned. In addition to his combat tours, in his role as a Navy Special Warfare Training Officer, Hiner was responsible for the shaping, training, and qualifying of hundreds of Navy SEALs. He has trained students at the Basic Underwater Demolition/SEAL (BUD/S) school; he has trained the trainers who train the students; he has been the officer in charge of training at the BUD/S school; and he has managed all basic and advanced training for West Coast SEAL Teams, and then for all Navy SEALs. He has trained all SEAL Team members to be leaders. He is among the most experienced SEAL trainers in the history of the organization.

He now offers up this vast experience base in his work as a coach and consultant specializing in leadership, team building, mental toughness, resilience, and personal conflict resolution.

He lives with his wife, Wendy, and son, Jake, in La Jolla, California.